Nourishing Noodles

SPIRALIZE Nearly 100 Plant-Based Recipes for
Zoodles, Ribbons, and Vegetable Spirals

CHRIS ANCA,
CREATOR OF *TALES OF A KITCHEN*

Race Point
PUBLISHING

Quarto is the authority on a wide range of topics.

Quarto educates, entertains and enriches the lives of our readers—enthusiasts and lovers of hands-on living.

www.quartoknows.com

First published in the United States of America in 2016 by
Race Point Publishing, a member of
Quarto Publishing Group USA Inc.
142 West 36th Street, 4th Floor
New York, New York 10018
www.quartoknows.com

10 9 8 7 6 5 4 3 2 1

ISBN 978-1-63106-184-4

Names: Anca, Chris, author.
Title: Nourishing noodles : nearly 100 plant-based recipes for spiralized
  zoodles, ribbons, and other vegetable spirals / Chris Anca.
Description: New York : Race Point Publishing, 2016. | Includes index.
Identifiers: LCCN 2016001713 | ISBN 9781631061844 (softbound)
Subjects: LCSH: Cooking (Vegetables) | LCGFT: Cookbooks.
Classification: LCC TX801 .A67 2016 | DDC 641.6/5--dc23
LC record available at http://lccn.loc.gov/2016001713

Editorial Director: Jeannine Dillon
Managing Editor: Erin Canning
Project Editor: Jason Chappell
Cover and Interior Design: Jacqui Caulton

Printed in China

Photo on page 31 © Shutterstock/Tobik
Dividers © Shutterstock/Olya Fedorovski
Background on pages ii, iii, 1, 13, 35, 47, 79, 80, 113, and 129 © Shutterstock/P. Chinnapong
Background on pages 4, 37, 38, 48, 63, 76, 97, 106, and 107 © iStockphoto/rusm
Background on pages 66 and 124 © Shutterstock/Bloomua

CONTENTS

INTRODUCTION

I love to eat, especially food that makes me happy (emotionally and physically), food that nourishes my body, and food that leaves me energized, without worrying about counting calories or fats or grams. To me, eating whole foods and superfoods, including heaps of fruits, veggies, whole grains, and nuts and seeds, and choosing organic when possible, equals abundance and a happy, humming body. It's a way of celebrating life, all around and within. And thanks to the invention of the spiralizer (seriously, how did I ever live without it?!), it is much easier to incorporate even more veggies and fruits into my diet and achieve my healthy-eating goals.

My diet is comprised mostly of plant-based foods. The majority of my meals are raw and/or vegan, so the recipes in this book fall into those categories. But you don't have to live a vegan, vegetarian, or raw lifestyle to enjoy these recipes. You just need two things: a spiralizer and a desire to add fresh, healthy, delicious, and comforting dishes to your menu. Turning your fruits and veggies into noodles takes just a few minutes with a spiralizer, so these recipes are also quick and easy to make for any night of the week.

I'm neither a professional chef nor an accredited dietitian. I'm a self-taught home cook, leading a healthy, active lifestyle (I run and run and run!), and I'm developing new recipes all the time. Sometimes I fail in the kitchen and at other times I succeed in making the perfect food. My recipes are not complicated and I find that they're also fun to make. And if I can make them, then so can you!

— Chris Anca

GETTING STARTED

The fact that you have picked up this book and are reading it means that you already have an interest in healthy and delicious recipes—and are most likely a noodle enthusiast or soon-to-become noodle enthusiast.

If you're a beginner at spiralizing, or cooking in general, this book is for you. The recipes are easy to make, with clear instructions and beautiful photos of the finished dishes. Many of the recipes are raw, and these are often the easiest to tackle in the kitchen, since you don't need to worry about timing or baking to precision. If you are already a savvy spiralizer, or a pro at cooking, I think you will still find inspiration among these pages and learn a thing or two about creating incredible meals that are entirely plant-based.

Most importantly, this book is filled with delicious, vibrant recipes that everyone can actually make, even at the end of a very busy day.

WHY ZOODLES, RIBBONS, AND SPIRALS?

Because spiralizing is easy to do, and I eat vegetable noodles almost daily in one form or another—and they're good for you. If you need further convincing, here are a number of reasons why I love zoodles, ribbons, and spirals and so should you:

- You want to include more veggies and fruits in your diet and you don't know how.
- You want to rely less on processed ingredients or refined white grains, such as pasta or white rice noodles.
- You're tired after a long day of work and want a quick, easy, nourishing dinner.
- You are gluten intolerant.
- You want more color on your plate.
- You want a meal that's fun to eat and bursting with fresh flavors.
- You want to skip slicing, dicing, and grating in the kitchen.
- You want to prepare a fun, healthy dinner with and for your kids.
- You want to create meals to impress your guests.

THE RECIPES

The recipes in this book are raw and/or vegan, so they are gluten-free, plant-based, and delicious, and include breakfast foods, appetizers and snacks, soups, entrées, and even desserts. Whether you're vegetarian, vegan, a noodle enthusiast, or simply trying to eat more plants, these recipes are a great way to create delicious meals that are also good for you. They are chock-full of freshness, color, and life. A lot of them require minimum preparation, but some do need a bit more time for soaking, boiling, dehydrating, pickling, or marinating.

I have also included a chapter for homemade basics and pantry staples (see page 129) that you can make from scratch, for a fraction of the cost of store-bought versions, including nut milks, vegan cheeses, spice blends, and condiments. These recipes will further help you eliminate the bad things usually found in store-bought products, and they will also help you appreciate your food even more. The satisfaction that you will feel when diving into that first jar of homemade kimchi is greater than can be put into words.

EATING SEASONALLY, LOCALLY, AND ORGANICALLY

As you cook your way through this cookbook, try to use ingredients that are seasonal, local, and organic. Choose foods that are abundantly available to you, foods that are picked at their ripest, and foods that don't travel long distances. And don't be afraid to make substitutions in the recipes.

Choosing to eat in this way is better for you, for local farmers, and for our planet. Plus, it will save you time in the kitchen—there is no need to peel your organic carrots or apples; just give them a quick rinse and use them whole. At the same time, I am well aware that organic produce can be more expensive and at times out of budget. Whatever and however much you can afford to buy organic is perfect. If you want to prioritize, the Environmental Working Group's Dirty Dozen™ and Clean 15™ lists (www.ewg.org/foodnews) are good starting points.

Eating with the seasons can also save you a penny or two—as fruits and veggies are at their cheapest when in season and in abundance. Buy bulk whenever you can and build a secret stash of goodies in the freezer or pantry. Freeze berries and chilies; dehydrate mango, apple, and pear slices; dehydrate herbs, tomatoes, and carrots; make tomato juice; and preserve lemons or freeze them.

STOCKING THE PANTRY

Here are the items I always have on-hand in my pantry—items that help me whip up simple, whole-food meals at home, no matter how tired I am at the end of the day or how little time I have.

As you gradually introduce these items into your home and replace the typical refined flours, grains, and sugar and prepackaged snacks, your pantry will transform your kitchen into an entirely new place and your body will feel the difference.

Oils and Vinegars

For salads, dips, spreads, or as garnish to a finished meal, I use cold-pressed extra virgin olive oil and cold-pressed sesame oil. Occasionally, I also buy a small bottle of cold-pressed avocado, hemp, or walnut oil—these need to be stored in the refrigerator as they tend to go rancid quite fast after opening (around a month or two); I buy as much as I need and use it up.

I use coconut oil almost exclusively for cooking. I find it to be perfect for sautéing, roasting, and baking—basically anything on the stove top or in the oven. There are plenty of varieties on the market, from those that are cold pressed with a strong flavor and taste to those that are refined, flavorless, and odorless. Choose one that suits your taste buds. I personally don't mind the tropical coconut flavor in my food, so I tend to choose a cold-pressed variety.

I keep two types of vinegar in my pantry: balsamic vinegar and raw apple cider vinegar. I make apple cider vinegar myself, but when I run out in between batches, I buy an organic, unfiltered version (with the mother).

Dried Legumes and Whole Grains

Cannellini beans, black beans, kidney beans, du Puy lentils, chickpeas, brown rice, wild rice, quinoa, and buckwheat, to name a few, are some of my favorite ways to bulk up meals and add fiber, protein, and nutrients. They are quite inexpensive, too, and have a long shelf life so they can be bought in bulk and stored in airtight containers. In addition to dried legumes, I always keep an "emergency" stash of a couple of cans of organic precooked chickpeas or lentils in the pantry for when I haven't had time to soak the dried beans in advance.

Nuts and Seeds

I'm nuts for nuts! And seeds. I always have at least two-to-three types of nuts and seeds in the pantry at any given time, as they make a great, satiating snack when cravings kick in. Almonds, cashews, pecans, walnuts, Brazil nuts, linseeds, sesame seeds, pumpkin seeds, sunflower seeds, and chia seeds (of course!) are some of my favorites.

Store-bought roasted nuts and seeds are often deep-fried and loaded with sugars and salt and other bad things, which defeat the purpose of a whole-food snack and does more harm than good. Choose nuts and seeds that are organic and raw, without any oils, salt, seasonings, or funky additives. Use them as is, or soak, toast, or roast them at home.

The natural oils in nuts and seeds tend to go rancid in a few months (from one to six), depending on the type of seed or nut, so if buying them from the bulk section, I highly recommend tasting one before purchasing. This is especially true for walnuts and pistachios, which you are better off buying in the shell.

Seasonings

Though I try to use the freshest ingredients whenever possible, I am not opposed to using dried seasonings in my recipes. My pantry is stocked with typical, easy-to-find spices, along with nutritional yeast. I also enjoy blending my own spice mixes, including curry powder (page 137), turmeric dukkah (page 141), veggie stock powder (page 153), and za'atar (page 156).

Sweeteners

My preferred natural sweeteners are dates, maple syrup, raw honey, coconut sugar, and fresh fruits, such as ripe bananas, where the recipe allows. These are better alternatives for sweetening foods than white, processed sugars, but they are still sweeteners and should be used moderately.

EQUIPMENT

Listed below are some of the cooking tools and appliances I use. While it's great having all of these items in the kitchen, you don't need all of them to begin your own healthy cooking journey.

Spiralizer

My spiralizer was love at first use. And while a relatively recent addition to my kitchen, I use it so frequently that I feel like I've had it forever. You will need one to make the recipes in this book and any other noodles you desire. It can also be used in a simpler manner to fancy up salads. I use a Three-in-One Spiral Vegetable Slicer. I find it easy to use and clean.

Blender and Food Processor

My Vitamix® blender is my best friend and my most treasured asset. From making smoothies, soups (cooked and raw), sauces, and creams to raw desserts, flours, and nut and seed butters, it does it all for me, reliably and fast.

I use a Breville® food processor and I love it. If you're not ready for a blender, make friends with a good food processor. You can make soups, sauces, creams, some raw desserts, dips, and hummus, and it will grind nuts and seeds.

Dehydrator

I use a 5 Tray Excalibur® with a timer. It's a great machine for making raw bread and crackers, raw cookies, raw wraps, fruit and veggie chips, raw vegetable stock powder, cheese wheels, and more. It also dries nuts and seeds after soaking. I would recommend this type of dehydrator with trays rather than a circular one, as I find the latter has a more limited use. If you don't have a dehydrator, you can use your oven on the lowest setting with the door ajar for most of the recipes in this book that call for one.

Cookware and More

A good casserole dish, stock pot, and a couple of heavy-duty saucepans go a long way to help you create beautiful soups and sauces, as well as to sauté and caramelize.

I use a Tiger rice cooker to cook brown rice, quinoa, millet, and buckwheat. It's easy to use, I don't have to keep an eye on it, and it acts as a warmer until I'm ready to eat. I also use it to steam veggies, if serving them with the whole grains.

Other items that make my life in the kitchen much easier are a veggie/fruit peeler, a mandolin for slicing and dicing, and a set of sharp knives.

HOW TO SPIRALIZE

As with any appliance, carefully read and follow the instructions provided with your spiralizer for proper use and care. The recipes in this book use the three basic blades for making ribbons (blade A); thick fettuccine-like noodles, or thick spirals, (blade B); and thin spaghetti-like noodles, or thin spirals, (blade C). Here are the simple steps to follow to start spiralizing:

1   Prep your veggies and fruits. Always wash produce well, then remove ends, slicing flat and evenly. Cut longer produce, such as zucchini, in half. (Regarding specific produce types, see Preparation and Spiralizing Tips below for additional instructions.)
2   Secure your spiralizer to the counter.
3   Choose your blade.
4   Attach your prepped veggie or fruit to the spiralizer. Align the center of one end of the produce with the center of the blade being used. Press the produce into the blade and press the handle of the spiralizer into the other end of the veggie or fruit until the teeth secure it in place. (Regarding specific produce types, see Preparation and Spiralizing Tips below for additional instructions.)
5   Spiralize!

PREPARATION AND SPIRALIZING TIPS

If the produce is organic, you can leave the skin on; if you are using conventional produce, I would recommend peeling before spiralizing. This does not apply to those vegetables in which it is always recommended to discard the peel, such as some root vegetables that have tough, thick skins. Here is a list of produce that is used in recipes in this book, with additional tips and tricks for successful spiralizing.

Apple — For best results, choose firm fruit. Do not worry about the core; it will go through the center of the blade, separate from the noodles.

Beet — To remove all of the dirt, scrub beets or even peel them before spiralizing.

Broccoli stalk — Peel and trim the knobby bits. Apply pressure when spiralizing, as it is firm.

Cabbage — Spiralizing cabbage is a quick, easy, and fun way to shred cabbage for salads or slaw, or to use in cooking. Choose a small-to-medium cabbage. Remove outer leaves and chop off the base. Secure the bottom of the cabbage onto the spiralizer flat blade (you can only spiralize cabbage on a flat blade).

Cantaloupe — Cantaloupes are not the easiest to spiralize, but the result is beautiful and fun. Halve the melon and scoop out and discard the seeds. Remove the rind of the melon, then cut melon into large chunks, trying to get them as flat and uniform as possible. Spiralize one piece at a time, applying very gentle pressure.

Carrot — Choose carrots that are thicker, at least ¾ inch (2 cm) in diameter. If your carrot has a thinner half, slice if off and only use the thicker half to obtain beautiful spirals.

Celeriac — Choose smaller celeriac to spiralize; the larger ones can be too firm and thick for the spiralizer to do a good job. Remove all of the thick, hairy, knobby outer skin. Apply pressure when spiralizing, as it is firm.

Chayote — Apply very gentle pressure when spiralizing, as chayote are very watery.

Cucumber — Apply very gentle pressure when spiralizing, as cucumbers are very watery.

Daikon — These are very easy to spiralize and have no additional instruction.

Kohlrabi — If it is a mature kohlrabi, peel it completely. If you're working with a baby kohlrabi, simply trim the knobby bits. Apply pressure when spiralizing, as it is firm.

Mango — Mangoes are not easy to spiralize, so the recipe must be worth it. Choose a firm, ripe mango. Gently peel it, then secure one of the flat sides onto the spiralizer blade. Apply gentle pressure to spiralize. When reaching the pit, turn the mango around and repeat on the other side. There will be leftover mango bits that cannot be spiralized; simply slice them off and use them as the recipe calls for.

Onion, red — Like cabbage, spiralizing onion is a quick and easy way to prepare it for cooking, with less tears. Choose a medium-to-large onion. Peel the outer skin, slice off the ends, and spiralize.

Parsnip — Choose parsnips that are thicker, at least ¾ inch (2 cm) in diameter. If your parsnip has a thinner half, slice if off and only use the thicker half to obtain beautiful spirals.

Pear — For best results, use firm fruit. Apply very gentle pressure when spiralizing, as pears have high water content and can lead to excess juices. Do not worry about the core; it will go through the center of the blade, separate from the noodles.

Potato, russet — Peel before spiralizing.

Potato, sweet — Peel them or wash them well if organic. If the sweet potato is too large or long, cut it in half and then spiralize.

Radish — Choose larger radishes for best results.

Rutabaga — Peel before spiralizing.

Squash, butternut — Choose smaller, thinner squash. Remove the tough skin before spiralizing. Secure the thinner edge onto the spiralizer blade and apply firm pressure. If your squash is thick, you can only spiralize until you reach the fleshy, seedy core. If your squash is extra long, cut it in half. Also, the seeds will separate from the noodles, remaining behind the blade.

Squash, dumpling — Remove the tough skin before spiralizing. Apply pressure when spiralizing, as it is firm. Also, the seeds will separate from the noodles, remaining behind the blade.

Squash, yellow — These are very easy to spiralize and have no additional instruction.

Turnip — Peel before spiralizing.

Zucchini — These are very easy to spiralize and have no additional instruction.

BREAKFASTS

Daily Greens Smoothie Bowl 2

Blueberry Smoothie Bowl 4

Carrot Granola Breakfast To-Go 7

Mango Kheer 8

Ginger-Pear Breakfast Bowl 9

Summer Melon Salad 11

DAILY GREENS SMOOTHIE BOWL

Serves 1

SMOOTHIE

1 cup (235 ml) Nut Milk (page 132), plus an extra ½ cup (120 ml), if needed, to blend well

1 kale leaf

6 mint leaves

1-inch (2.5 cm) piece ginger

1 frozen banana, cut into chunks (peel and cut before freezing)

1 slice lemon, peeled and seeded

½ seasonal apple

3 tbsp homemade chia pudding or 1 tbsp chia seeds

1 tsp spirulina

NOODLES

⅓ Lebanese cucumber, thin spirals

1 small Granny Smith apple, thin spirals

TOPPINGS

½ cup (61 g) unsweetened granola

4–5 raspberries

2–3 lime slices

4–5 almonds (or nut of your choice)

2–3 mint leaves

1 Place all smoothie ingredients in a blender and process until smooth.

2 Transfer to a medium bowl. Add the cucumber and apple noodles to the bowl.

3 Top with granola, raspberries, lime, almonds, and mint, and serve immediately.

BLUEBERRY SMOOTHIE BOWL

Serves 1

NOODLES
⅓ medium beet, thin spirals

⅓ medium carrot, thin spirals

Juice of ½ orange

SMOOTHIE
1 cup (235 ml) Nut Milk (page 132),
plus an extra ½ cup (120 ml),
if needed, to blend well

2 frozen bananas, cut into chunks
(peel and cut before freezing)

¼–⅓ cup (40–50 g) blueberries

½ orange, peeled, seeded, and
roughly chopped

2–3 small dates, pitted

1 tbsp chia seeds

½ tsp ground cinnamon

TOPPINGS
½ cup (61 g) granola or oats

½ blood orange, sliced

1 small handful blueberries

2–3 pecans or almonds

1 tbsp hemp hearts

1 Add all noodle ingredients to a small-to-medium bowl and massage for 30 seconds to soften noodles. Set aside.

2 Place all smoothie ingredients in a blender and process until smooth. Transfer to a separate medium bowl.

3 Add the noodles and toppings to the smoothie bowl and serve.

CARROT GRANOLA BREAKFAST TO-GO

Serves 1

NOODLES

⅓ medium carrot, thin spirals

⅓ medium sweet dumpling squash, thin noodles

3–4 tbsp fresh lemon juice

⅓ tsp ground cinnamon

¼ tsp coconut sugar

GRANOLA

3 tbsp coconut chips

2 tbsp almonds

2 tbsp pecans

2 tbsp rolled oats

1 tbsp goji berries

2–3 tbsp leftover grated carrot from spiralizing noodles

½ tsp ground cinnamon

TOPPINGS

1 cup (245 g) yogurt or the blended flesh of 1 young coconut

1 pinch vanilla seeds

½ tsp maple syrup

1 pinch ground cinnamon

1 pinch coconut sugar

1 pinch ground turmeric

1 Place all noodle ingredients in a medium bowl. Gently massage for 30 seconds and set aside.

2 To make the carrot granola, place the coconut chips, almonds, pecans, oats, and goji berries in a food processor and process until combined and crumbled.

3 Transfer the nut mix to a medium bowl and toss with grated carrot and cinnamon.

4 If you are using a young coconut to top your granola, add the flesh to a blender with ½ cup (120 ml) coconut water from the young coconut, vanilla seeds, and maple syrup. Process until very smooth.

5 To assemble, add the noodle mixture to the bottom of a 16-oz (500 ml) jar. Top with granola, followed by the coconut cream or yogurt. Finish with a dusting of cinnamon, coconut sugar, and turmeric, and serve.

Tip: You can prepare this breakfast the day before and store it in the refrigerator overnight. The flavors will have time to infuse and it will taste even better the next day.

MANGO KHEER

Serves 2

KHEER

2 cups (475 ml) warm Coconut Milk (page 133) or store-bought organic coconut milk

Leftover mango flesh that could not be spiralized (see Noodles below)

1 pinch saffron threads

1 pinch ground turmeric

NOODLES

1 large mango, thick spirals (mango should be ripe but still firm)

TOPPINGS

1 tbsp pistachios

$\frac{1}{3}$ tsp coconut sugar

1 pinch ground cinnamon

2 tbsp coconut flakes

1 Place all kheer ingredients in a blender and process until smooth.

2 Pour the kheer into serving bowls.

3 Add the mango noodles and toppings, and serve.

GINGER-PEAR BREAKFAST BOWL

Serves 2

SAUCE

Juice of ½ lime

Juice of ½ mandarin

¼ cup (60 ml) water

¼ cup (38 g) cashews

2 tbsp cold-pressed coconut oil

1 tsp coconut sugar

1 tsp chia seeds

1 pinch ground turmeric

⅓ tsp mesquite powder (optional)

NOODLES

2 firm Asian (nashi) pears, thin spirals

TOPPINGS

2 large handfuls of your favorite granola
(I always make my own toasted
coconut granola—an unsweetened
mix of coconut flakes, almonds,
pecans, cashews, sunflower seeds,
sesame seeds, and pepitas)

8 walnuts, crumbled

8 pecans, crumbled

1 tbsp hemp hearts

4 tbsp puffed quinoa

1 tbsp ginger snow (grated frozen ginger)

1   Place all sauce ingredients in a blender and
process until smooth and creamy. Set aside.

2   Place pear noodles in serving bowls.

3   Top noodles with sauce and toppings, and
serve immediately.

SUMMER MELON SALAD

Serves 2

DRESSING

2 tbsp coconut water

¼ cup (60 ml) fresh lime juice

1 tsp chia seeds

NOODLES

1 chilled cantaloupe, thick spirals
(cut melon into large chunks,
then gently press chunks into the
spiralizer blade)

TOPPINGS

2 large handfuls frozen blueberries

1 medium handful slivered almonds

½ orange, cut into wedges

1 lime, cut into wedges

1 small handful roughly torn mint leaves

2–3 sunflower sprouts

1 tsp chia seeds

Frozen Two-Ingredient Nice Cream chunks
(page 157) or frozen banana chunks

1 Place all dressing ingredients in a small bowl and
whisk to combine. Set aside for 10–15 minutes.

2 Place noodles in a large bowl and pour dressing
on top. Gently toss noodles until thoroughly coated.

3 Transfer noodles to a serving plate and add the
toppings.

4 When ready to serve, top with the frozen nice
cream or banana chunks and enjoy immediately.

APPETIZERS AND SNACKS

Green Wraps with Hummus 14

Fresh Spring Rolls with Maple Mustard Dipping Sauce 16

Zucchini and Tomato Noodle Pancakes 19

Squash, Tomato, and Cheese Canapés 20

Pear, Date, and Cheese Canapés 21

Curried Squash Noodle Rolls 22

Avocado Nori Rolls with Miso Dipping Sauce 24

Tempeh Nori Rolls with Miso Raspberry Dipping Sauce 26

Cheesy Quinoa Bites 28

Apple and Pear Chips 31

Celeriac Winter Fruit Salad 32

GREEN WRAPS WITH HUMMUS

Makes 4 wraps

CHICKPEA HUMMUS

1 15.5-oz (439 g) can organic cooked chickpeas, drained

¼ cup (60 g) hulled tahini

¼ cup (60 ml) fresh lemon juice or raw apple cider vinegar

6 tbsp cold-pressed extra virgin olive oil

1 medium garlic clove

½ tsp cumin seeds

½ tsp smoked paprika

½ tsp sea salt flakes

TAHINI HUMMUS (RAW)

½ cup (120 g) hulled tahini

½ cup (75 g) cashews

¼ cup (60 ml) water

¼ cup (60 ml) raw apple cider vinegar

6 tbsp cold-pressed extra virgin olive oil

1 medium garlic clove

½ tsp cumin seeds

½ tsp smoked paprika

½ tsp sea salt flakes

NOODLES

1 medium zucchini, thin spirals

2 medium carrots, thin spirals (reserve carrot greens)

6 large radishes, thin spirals

WRAPS

6 Swiss chard leaves or leafy green of choice (reserve stems and julienne them)

1 green bell pepper (capsicum), julienned

Carrot greens, to taste

Note: I've included two hummus recipes (one raw and one not raw), so you can use which one you prefer.

1 Place all ingredients for hummus of choice in a blender and process until smooth and creamy. Add a little water, 1–2 tablespoons at a time, if needed, to blend.

2 Lay Swiss chard leaves flat and fill one side with hummus and some of the zucchini, carrot, and radish noodles. Top the hummus with a few strips of green pepper, 2–3 carrot greens, and 2–3 Swiss chard strips.

3 Carefully wrap leaves to enclose ingredients.

4 Repeat steps 3–4 with the remaining Swiss chard leaves.

5 Serve with extra hummus for dipping.

Tip: These hummus recipes are basic and can be loaded with even more goodness. Two personal favorites of mine are hummus with roasted red pepper and hummus with greens and extra lemon.

FRESH SPRING ROLLS WITH MAPLE MUSTARD DIPPING SAUCE

Makes 5–6 spring rolls

NOODLES

⅓ medium carrot, thin spirals

1 tbsp raw apple cider vinegar

½ tsp raw honey or maple syrup

⅓ medium zucchini, thin spirals

½ Lebanese cucumber, thin spirals

DIPPING SAUCE

1 cup (150 g) cashews

½ cup (120 ml) water

2 tbsp Homemade Mustard (page 135)

2 tbsp maple syrup

1-inch (2.5 cm) piece green (spring) onion, white part only

¼ tsp sea salt flakes

¼ tsp garlic powder

¼ cup (60 ml) fresh lemon juice

1 pinch chili flakes

ROLLS

5–6 rice paper wrappers

1 avocado, halved, pitted, and sliced lengthwise

1 small handful sunflower sprouts

10–12 mint leaves

10–12 cilantro (coriander) leaves

1 Place carrot noodles in a large bowl. Add apple cider vinegar and raw honey or maple syrup to the bowl and massage noodles for 30 seconds. Add the zucchini and cucumber noodles to the bowl, next to the carrot noodles (do not mix noodles).

2 Place all dipping sauce ingredients in a blender and process until creamy and smooth. Pour into dipping bowls.

3   To make the rolls, dip the rice paper wrappers in cold water for 2–3 seconds, then place them on a clean, dry cutting board, rough sides up. Add a small handful of each of the noodles right below the center line and top with avocado, sprouts, mint, and cilantro.

4   Lift the side of the wrapper closer to you and tuck it tightly on top of the filling. Lift the sides of the sheet and tuck them tightly on top of the filing.

5   Begin to roll away from you, applying gentle pressure on the filling to keep everything in place; this pressure will help create a firm roll.

6   Repeat steps 4–5 for remaining rolls.

7   Serve immediately with dipping sauce on the side.

ZUCCHINI AND TOMATO NOODLE PANCAKES

Serves 4

NOODLES

2 medium Roma tomatoes

¼ cup (40 g) linseed meal

1 medium zucchini, thin spirals

½ tsp dried basil

½ tsp dried oregano

TOPPINGS (OPTIONAL OR TRY YOUR OWN)

1 avocado, halved, pitted, and sliced

1 large handful Dried Tomatoes (page 151)

4 cherry tomatoes, halved

1 small handful sunflower shoots

4 tsp tahini

4 lemon wedges

Chili flakes, to taste

Sea salt flakes, to taste

1 Add the tomatoes and linseed to a blender and process until smooth.

2 In a medium bowl, combine the blended tomatoes with the zucchini noodles and dried spices, and set aside for 15 minutes.

3 Divide the zucchini and tomato mixture into 4 equal parts and arrange them in pancake shapes on a dehydrator mesh tray. Keep your pancakes at least ¾ inch (2 cm) thick—don't worry, they will thin out.

4 Dehydrate at 125°F (52°C) for 2 hours, then lower the temperature to 115°F (46°C) until pancakes are crispy and dry. If you don't have a dehydrator, simply arrange the pancakes on a baking sheet lined with parchment paper and bake at the lowest temperature with the door ajar. Keep an eye on them as they will be ready in less than half the time required for dehydration.

5 Serve immediately with any of the optional toppings, or store in an airtight container in the refrigerator for a few days.

SQUASH, TOMATO, AND CHEESE CANAPÉS

Makes 10 canapés

NOODLES
½ pattypan squash, thin spirals

1 tsp raw apple cider vinegar

CANAPÉ BASES
10 rice crackers or cucumber slices

10 tsp Garlic and Chives Cream Cheese
(page 150), divided

TOPPINGS
2 Dried Tomatoes (page 151),
thinly sliced into 10 slices

5 Kalamata or green olives, pitted
and halved

10 basil leaves

1 Place the squash noodles in a medium bowl and
massage with the apple cider vinegar. Set aside.

2 Spread a teaspoon of cream cheese onto each rice
cracker or cucumber slice.

3 Top each base with 2–3 squash noodles, 1 dried
tomato slice, an olive half, and 1 basil leaf, and serve.

PEAR, DATE, AND CHEESE CANAPÉS

Makes 10 canapés

NOODLES

½ Asian (nashi) pear, thin noodles

1 tsp maple syrup

2 Medjool dates, pitted and sliced into 10 strips total

10 pecans

CANAPÉ BASES

10 rice or linseed crackers

10 tsp Garlic and Chives Cream Cheese (page 150), divided

1 Place the pear noodles in a medium bowl and massage with the maple syrup. Set aside.

2 Spread a teaspoon of cream cheese onto each cracker.

3 Top each base with 2–3 pear noodles, 1 strip of date, and 1 pecan, and serve.

CURRIED SQUASH NOODLE ROLLS

Makes 4 rolls

NOODLES

½ small butternut squash, thick spirals

1 tbsp Curry Sauce (see Curry-Lime
  Sweet Potato Noodles on page 90)

2 tbsp fresh lime juice

¼ tsp garlic powder

DIPPING SAUCE

1 tbsp tamari

½ tsp grated ginger

2 tbsp fresh lime juice

ROLLS

4 rice paper wrappers

4 orange slices, peeled and halved

8 mint leaves

1 small handful mixed cilantro (coriander)
  and parsley leaves

4 chives

4 tsp crushed almonds

1 Place all noodle ingredients in a large bowl and toss until thoroughly coated. Set aside.

2 Place all dipping sauce ingredients in a small bowl and whisk to combine. Set aside.

3 To make the rolls, dip the rice paper wrappers in cold water for 2–3 seconds, making sure the water wets both sides.

4 Place the wet wrappers on a cutting board, rough sides up. Add a few squash noodles, 2 orange slices, 2 mint leaves, 4–5 cilantro and parsley leaves, 1 chive, and 1 teaspoon crushed almonds below the center line of each wrapper.

5 Lift the side of the wrapper closer to you and tuck it tightly on top of the filling. Lift the sides of the sheet and tuck them tightly on top of the filling.

6 Begin to roll away from you, applying gentle pressure on the filling to keep everything in place; this pressure will help create a firm roll.

7 Repeat steps 5–6 to make the remaining rolls.

8 Serve with the dipping sauce and enjoy fresh.

AVOCADO NORI ROLLS WITH MISO DIPPING SAUCE

Makes 4 rolls

DIPPING SAUCE

1 heaping tsp white miso paste

2 tbsp hulled tahini

1 tsp grated ginger

1 tbsp raw apple cider vinegar

5 tbsp water

1 tsp coconut nectar or maple syrup

NOODLES

½ small yellow squash, thin spirals

⅓ medium carrot, thin spirals

⅕ medium daikon radish, thin spirals

ROLLS

1 small handful chopped iceberg, romaine, or butter lettuce

½ avocado, sliced

1 raw nori sheet

1 Place all dipping sauce ingredients in a small bowl and mix with a spoon until thick and creamy. Set aside.

2 Before making the rolls, arrange the prepped noodles, lettuce, and avocado on plates/cutting boards around the workspace. Also place a small bowl of water next to the ingredients.

3 To make the rolls, cover a bamboo rolling mat with cling wrap (this makes rolling easier and prevents the nori from sticking to the mat). Place the sheet of nori on the rolling mat, shiny side down.

4 Spread all noodles evenly over the nori sheet, leaving a ¾-inch (2 cm) strip uncovered along the edge farthest from you.

5 Arrange the lettuce and avocado right below the center of the nori sheet.

6 Keep your fingers on the filling to hold it in place and gently begin rolling by lifting the edge of the bamboo mat closest to you and folding in the roll. Continue to firmly press and fold, lifting the bamboo mat as you're rolling. If needed, to hold the roll together, moisten the edge of the nori sheet farther from you by dipping your finger in the prepared bowl of water and running it along the edge. Finish rolling and set aside for about 3 minutes.

7 Cut the roll into quarters and serve immediately with the miso dipping sauce.

TEMPEH NORI ROLLS WITH
MISO RASPBERRY DIPPING SAUCE

Makes 8 rolls

DIPPING SAUCE

1 tsp white miso paste

3 tbsp kimchi liquid from Napa
   Cabbage Kimchi (page 154)

1 small handful raspberries

1 tsp yuzu juice (or fresh lime juice)

2 tsp cold-pressed extra virgin
   olive oil

NOODLES

1 small carrot, thin spirals, divided

1 small, crisp Fiji apple, thin spirals,
   divided

ROLLS

½ block (4 oz/114 g) tempeh

2 finely chopped kale leaves

1 tbsp fresh lemon juice

2 raw nori sheets

2 large handfuls chopped iceberg,
   romaine, or butter lettuce

1 Place kale in a small bowl with the lemon juice. Massage gently for 1 minute, or until softened. Set aside.

2 Place all dipping sauce ingredients in a food processor and blend until smooth. Set aside.

3 Heat a grill pan over medium heat and add the tempeh. Cook for 4–5 minutes on each side, then remove from heat and set aside for 5–10 minutes to cool.

4 Once the tempeh is cool, cut it into 8 strips and set aside.

5 Before making the rolls, arrange the prepped noodles, tempeh, and kale on plates/cutting boards around the workspace. Also place a small bowl of water next to the ingredients.

6 To make the rolls, cover a bamboo rolling mat with cling wrap (this makes rolling easier and prevents the nori from sticking to the mat). Place a sheet of nori on the rolling mat, shiny side down.

7 Spread half of both noodles evenly over the nori sheet, leaving a ¾-inch (2-cm) strip uncovered along the edge farthest from you.

8 Arrange half each of the kale, lettuce, and sliced tempeh right below the center of the noodles.

9   Keep your fingers on the filling to hold it in place and gently begin rolling by lifting the edge of the bamboo mat closest to you and folding in the roll. Continue to firmly press and fold, lifting the bamboo mat as you're rolling. If needed, to hold the roll together, moisten the edge of the nori sheet farther from you by dipping your finger in the prepared bowl of water and running it along the edge. Finish rolling and set aside for about 3 minutes.

10 Repeat steps 6–9 with the remaining nori sheet.

11 Cut the rolls into quarters and serve immediately with the dipping sauce.

CHEESY QUINOA BITES

Makes 12 bites

QUINOA BITES

3 cups (550 g) cooked quinoa

1 small handful chopped parsley leaves

1 small handful chopped mint leaves

1 medium garlic clove, finely grated

½ cup (116 g) Garlic and Chives Cream Cheese (page 150), plus extra, if needed

5 tbsp (74 g) hulled tahini, plus extra, if needed

⅓ cup (80 ml) cold-pressed extra virgin olive oil

1 tsp sea salt flakes

½ tsp freshly cracked black pepper

NOODLES

½ medium carrot, thin spirals

1 small beet, thin spirals

1 large parsnip, thin spirals

1 Preheat dehydrator to 145°F (63°C) or oven on the lowest heat setting.

2 Place all ingredients for the quinoa bites in a large bowl.

3 Run a knife through the spiralized noodles a couple of times to cut them into smaller pieces.

4 Add noodles to the quinoa bites bowl and combine well. If the mix is not sticky enough to form into balls, add more cream cheese and tahini, a teaspoon at a time of each, until the dough is sticky enough.

5 Form 12 balls, arranging them on a dehydrator mesh tray, and dehydrate for 1½ hours. If using an oven, arrange them on a baking sheet lined with parchment paper and bake for 15–20 minutes, until the outside becomes slightly crispy.

6 These are best enjoyed warm, but also delicious when chilled.

APPLE AND PEAR CHIPS

Serves 3–4

SPICE MIX

Juice of 1 orange

½ cup (120 ml) water

1 tbsp ground cinnamon

DIPPING SAUCE

1 tbsp tamari

½ tsp grated ginger

2 tbsp fresh lime juice

NOODLES

3 seasonal apples, flat chips

3 seasonal, firm pears, flat chips

(score the apples and pears on one side only, along the core, then spiralize on the flat blade for perfectly round chips)

1 Preheat dehydrator to 125°F (52°C).

2 Place all spice mix ingredients in a large bowl and whisk to combine.

3 Add the apple chips to the spice mix as you spiralize them, to let them absorb the flavor and prevent oxidation. When apple chips are all in the bowl, toss gently to thoroughly cover them in the spice mix.

4 Arrange the apple chips on 2–3 dehydrator mesh trays, in a single layer, and place them in the dehydrator.

5 Repeat steps 3–4 with the pears—add to spice mix, toss, arrange on mesh trays and place in dehydrator.

6 After 1½ hours, lower the temperature to 100°F (42°C) and continue to dehydrate until the chips are dry and crispy.

7 Chips keep well in an airtight container for several weeks, though they are most delicious when just made!

Note: Depending on the type of dehydrator you're using, you may need to rotate the trays 180 degrees after 2–3 hours to ensure even drying of chips. Also, you might need to switch around trays—I noticed my chips dry faster on the middle trays and slower on the bottom and top. That's why, midway through, I rotate the trays as well.

CELERIAC WINTER FRUIT SALAD

Serves 2

NOODLES

½ medium celeriac, thick spirals

Juice of 1 mandarin

1 tsp Za'atar (page 156)

TOPPINGS

1 mandarin, peeled, seeded, and cubed

1 tbsp currants

Pomegranate seeds of ½ pomegranate, divided

8–10 mint leaves, roughly torn, divided

¼ cup (25 g) chopped pistachios (lightly toasted if you prefer)

1 Place all noodle ingredients in a medium bowl and massage to thoroughly coat and soften.

2 Add cubed mandarin, currants, and half each of the pomegranate seeds and mint leaves, and toss to thoroughly mix.

3 Place the noodles in serving bowls, top with pistachios and the remaining pomegranate and mint, and serve immediately.

SOUPS

Vegan Laksa 37

Caramelized Pumpkin Soup with
Curry Sweet Potato Noodles 39

Quick Miso Noodle Soup 43

Ginger-Lime Coconut Soup 44

VEGAN LAKSA

Serves 4

LAKSA PASTE

1 tbsp coriander seeds

1 tbsp cumin seeds

5 cilantro (coriander) roots and stalks (reserve leaves)

3 fresh chilies of your choice (as hot as you want them), stemmed and seeded, if you prefer (I use them whole)

4 red shallots, peeled and roughly chopped

1-inch (2.5 cm) piece ginger, roughly chopped

3 large garlic cloves, quartered

2 large lemongrass stalks (white parts only), trimmed and roughly chopped

1 medium handful cashews

1 tsp paprika

1 tbsp turmeric (you can use freshly grated or dried powder)

5 tbsp tomato paste

SOUP

¼ cup (60 ml) cold-pressed coconut oil

85 oz (2.5 L) vegetable stock

1 tbsp coconut sugar

1¾ cups (400 ml) Coconut Milk (page 133) or 1 13.5-oz can organic coconut milk

5 kaffir lime leaves

2 tbsp tamari or soy sauce

NOODLES

1 medium zucchini, thin spirals

2 medium carrots, thin spirals

3 button mushroom caps, thinly sliced

10 sugar snap peas, thinly sliced

4 small handfuls bean sprouts

1 green (spring) onion, thinly sliced

TOPPINGS

1 large handful cilantro (coriander) leaves

1 fresh chili, thinly sliced, to taste (or chili flakes)

4 lime wedges

1 Place coriander and cumin seeds in a small saucepan and place over low heat. Lightly toast for 1–2 minutes, being careful not to burn them. Set aside and allow to cool for a few minutes.

2 Once cooled, add the seeds to a mortar and pestle and grind them to a fine powder.

3 Place the remaining ingredients for the laksa paste in a food processor and blend until you get a fine paste, approximately 1 minute. Transfer to a small bowl and set aside.

4 Heat a large saucepan over medium-high heat. Add the laksa paste and coconut oil, and cook for 2–3 minutes, stirring, until hot and fragrant.

5 Add the remaining soup ingredients to the saucepan. Stir, cover, and bring to a boil. Lower the heat and simmer for 10 minutes, covered.

6 Divide the noodle ingredients among the serving bowls, carefully arranging each ingredient next to each other: zucchini noodles, carrot noodles, sliced mushrooms, sliced sugar snap peas, bean sprouts, and green onions.

7 When the soup is ready, scoop 3–4 ladles into each serving bowl.

8 Top with fresh cilantro, chili flakes, a squeeze of fresh lime juice, and serve hot.

CARAMELIZED PUMPKIN SOUP WITH CURRY SWEET POTATO NOODLES

Serves 4

SOUP

5 pumpkin wedges (roughly ½ medium Jarrahdale pumpkin or kabocha)

3 tbsp cold-pressed coconut oil, divided

1 medium red onion, roughly chopped

4 medium garlic cloves, roughly chopped

¾-inch (2 cm) piece ginger, thinly sliced

¾-inch (2 cm) piece turmeric root, thinly sliced

1 tsp cumin seeds

1 cinnamon stick

1 tsp chili flakes (or to taste)

1¾ cups (400 ml) Coconut Milk (page 133) or 1 13.5-oz can organic coconut milk

1 cup (240 ml) water

1 14.5-oz (411 g) can organic whole tomatoes

3 tbsp Veggie Stock Powder (page 153)

1 tsp sea salt flakes

½ tsp freshly cracked black pepper

TOASTED SEEDS

½ cup (113 g) sunflower seeds

½ cup (113 g) pepitas

NOODLES

2 tbsp cold-pressed coconut oil

1 sweet potato, thick spirals

1 tsp paprika

1 tsp Curry Powder (page 137)

½ tsp sea salt flakes

⅓ tsp freshly cracked black pepper

TOPPINGS

¼ cup (60 ml) hulled tahini

2 tbsp balsamic vinegar

½ green (spring) onion, thinly sliced

1 red chili, finely chopped

2 tbsp fresh thyme

1 Preheat oven to 375°F (190°C).

2 Massage the pumpkin wedges with 2 tablespoons coconut oil and bake for 40 minutes, or until tender and caramelized. Remove from the oven and allow to cool.

3 While the pumpkin is baking, heat 1 tablespoon coconut oil in a medium stockpot over medium heat. Add the onion and cook until translucent.

4 Add the garlic, ginger, turmeric, cumin, cinnamon stick, and chili flakes and cook for approximately 4 minutes, stirring, until fragrant.

5 Add the coconut milk, water, and tomatoes to the stockpot and stir.

6 Bring to a boil, then add veggie stock powder, 1 teaspoon salt, and ½ teaspoon pepper, lower the heat, and simmer, covered, about 15 minutes.

7 Add sunflower seeds and pepitas to a small pan and lightly toast 3–4 minutes on low-medium heat, stirring often so they don't burn. Transfer to a bowl and set aside to cool.

8 Remove soup from heat and allow to cool. Discard the cinnamon stick.

9 Roughly chop 4 pumpkin wedges into smaller pieces and thinly slice the remaining wedge.

10 Add some of the chopped pumpkin to a blender with 1–2 ladles of soup. Purée until smooth, then add to a large pot. Repeat this step until you have puréed all of the pumpkin and soup.

11 Place the puréed soup over medium heat.

12 Heat 2 tablespoons coconut oil in a large saucepan over medium-high heat. Add the sweet potato noodles to the pan with the paprika, curry powder, salt, and pepper. Cook for about 10 minutes, or until crispy.

13 Ladle the soup into serving bowls. Top each bowl with 1–2 slices of roasted pumpkin, a handful of curry sweet potato noodles, tahini, balsamic vinegar, green onion, chili, thyme, and generous amounts of toasted seeds. Serve hot.

QUICK MISO NOODLE SOUP

Serves 4

STOCK
15 dried shiitake mushrooms
4 cups (950 ml) hot water

NOODLES
1 tbsp cold-pressed coconut oil
1 tsp cold-pressed sesame oil
1 small daikon radish, thick spirals
1 small-to-medium sweet potato,
    thick spirals
1 tbsp sake
2 tbsp white or red miso paste
1 tsp Fermented Hot Chili Sauce
    (page 138)

TOPPINGS
1 spring onion, thinly sliced
2 tbsp white and/or black sesame seeds,
    lightly toasted (page 131)

1 Place the dried shiitake mushrooms and hot water in a medium-to-large pot. Cover and set aside for 1 hour.

2 Drain the mushrooms, reserving the liquid as stock for the soup. Set aside. Place the shiitake mushrooms in a jar and refrigerate (you can pickle them as per the Sweet-and-Sour Pickled Shiitake recipe on page 152 and use in a lot of other dishes).

3 Heat the coconut oil in a medium-to-large saucepan over medium heat. Add the sesame oil and daikon and sweet potato noodles to the pan. Sauté for about 5 minutes, stirring occasionally so the noodles cook evenly.

4 Add the sake and continue cooking for 1–2 minutes.

5 Add all of the mushroom stock and bring to a boil. Lower the heat and simmer for 5–10 minutes, or until the noodles are cooked but still firm.

6 Remove from heat and stir in the miso and chili sauce.

7 Ladle the soup into serving bowls, top with spring onion and sesame seeds, and serve hot.

GINGER-LIME COCONUT SOUP

Serves 2

SOUP

¼ cup (60 ml) cold-pressed coconut oil

3 green (spring) onions, roughly chopped

¾-inch (2 cm) piece ginger, roughly
   chopped

¾-inch (2 cm) piece galangal (you
   can substitute with more ginger),
   roughly chopped

5 cilantro (coriander) plants, roots
   (whole), stalks (roughly chopped),
   and leaves (reserve)

1 yellow bell pepper (capsicum),
   roughly chopped

Chili flakes, to taste

1¾ cups (400 ml) Coconut Milk (page 133)
   or 1 13.5-oz can organic coconut milk

2 cups (475 ml) water

2 tsp sea salt flakes

NOODLES

½ medium sweet potato, thin spirals

½ medium-to-large zucchini, thin spirals

TOPPINGS

1 large handful cilantro (coriander) leaves

2 tbsp chopped chives

1 fresh chili, finely chopped, to taste

2 lime wedges

1 small handful enoki mushrooms
   (optional)

1 Heat the coconut oil in a large saucepan on
   medium-high heat. Add the green onions, ginger,
   galangal, and coriander roots and stalks, stirring,
   and cook until fragrant.

2 Add the yellow bell pepper and chili flakes and
   cook for an additional 3–4 minutes.

3 Add the coconut milk, water, and sea salt to the
   saucepan, stir, and bring to a boil.

4 Lower the heat and simmer for 15 minutes, covered.

5 Place noodles in serving bowls.

6 When the soup is ready, strain it (reserve the
   ginger, galangal, coriander stalks, and yellow
   pepper, if it is to your taste, and add them back
   into the soup), then discard the remnants.

7 Pour the hot soup over the noodles, add the
   toppings, and serve hot.

RAW ENTRÉES

Cucumber and Sprouts Thai Noodle Salad 48

Heirloom Carrot Noodle Salad with Mustard Avocado Dressing 50

Beet, Zucchini, and Apple Noodle Salad 53

Ranch Noodle Salad with BBQ Almonds 54

Apple Noodle Salad with Cabbage, Dill, and Miso Mayo 56

"Bacon," Lettuce, and Tomato Noodles 58

Beet, Carrot, and Cabbage Salad with Goji Miso Dressing 59

Thai-Inspired Carrot Noodles with Ginger-Lime
Coconut Dressing 60

Zucchini Noodles with Kale Pesto 63

Beet and Herb Noodles with Preserved Lemon 64

Raw Zucchini Marinara 66

Four Noodles Super Bowl 68

Turnip Noodles with Za'atar, Preserved Lemon,
and "Yogurt" Dressing 70

Mixed Root Vegetables with Avocado Dressing 73

Purple Carrot Noodles with Thai Coconut Sauce 74

Carrot Noodles with Zesty Garlic Sauce 75

Miso Kohlrabi Noodles with Coconut Bacon 76

CUCUMBER AND SPROUTS
THAI NOODLE SALAD

Serves 2 (as a light meal)

DRESSING

1 tbsp tamari

Juice and pulp of ½ lime

1 tbsp coconut nectar

½ tsp grated ginger

¼ tsp cold-pressed sesame oil

½ tsp chia seeds

1 pinch chili flakes

NOODLES

2 large handfuls sunflower sprouts

4 small radishes, thinly sliced

2 small handfuls finely chopped mint

1 small spring onion, thinly sliced

2 Lebanese cucumbers, thin spirals

SERVING/TOPPINGS

2 large handfuls baby spinach or
   seasonal greens of your choice

1 tbsp white and/or black sesame seeds

2 lime wedges

1 Place all dressing ingredients in a large bowl and whisk to combine.

2 Add the sprouts, radish, mint, and onion to the dressing bowl and toss until thoroughly coated. Massage vegetables for about 1 minute to help soften them. Let sit for 5 minutes.

3 Add cucumber noodles to the bowl and toss until thoroughly coated.

4 Arrange a large handful of baby spinach or greens of choice on each plate, then top with coated noodles.

5 Sprinkle on sesame seeds and serve with lime wedges.

HEIRLOOM CARROT NOODLE SALAD WITH MUSTARD AVOCADO DRESSING

Serves 2 (as a light meal)

NOODLES

3 large heirloom carrots, thin spirals
(I used 1 yellow, 1 orange, and
1 purple carrot)

DRESSING

½ avocado

1 tbsp Homemade Mustard (page 135)

⅓ cup (80 ml) cold-pressed extra
virgin olive oil

2 tbsp raw apple cider vinegar

½ tsp sea salt flakes

¼ tsp freshly cracked black pepper

1 pinch chili flakes

TOPPINGS

1 small handful roughly chopped
cilantro (coriander)

2 tbsp Turmeric Dukkah (page 141)

1 small handful alfalfa sprouts

1 Place carrot noodles in a large bowl.

2 Place all dressing ingredients in a blender and
process until smooth.

3 Add dressing to the noodles and toss until
thoroughly coated.

4 Top with cilantro, turmeric dukkah, and alfalfa
sprouts, and serve.

BEET, ZUCCHINI, AND APPLE NOODLE SALAD

Serves 1

NOODLES

1 medium apple, thick spirals
 (any seasonal apple will work)

1 tbsp fresh lemon juice

½ medium zucchini, thin spirals

½ medium beet, thin spirals

DRESSING

¼ cup (60 ml) cold-pressed extra
 virgin olive oil

1 tbsp raw apple cider vinegar

1 tbsp fresh lemon juice

1 heaping tsp Homemade Mustard
 (page 135)

1 small garlic clove

1 small handful macadamia nuts

20 snow pea sprouts

SERVING/TOPPINGS

1 large handful mustard greens

2 tbsp crushed almonds

1 tbsp fresh thyme

1 Place apple noodles in a large bowl and add the lemon juice. Toss until coated to prevent browning.

2 Add the zucchini and beet noodles to the bowl.

3 Place all dressing ingredients in a blender and process until it becomes creamy and smooth.

4 Add the dressing to the noodles, toss, and gently massage until thoroughly coated and softened.

5 Place mustard greens on plate, then top with noodles, crushed almonds, and thyme.

RANCH NOODLE SALAD WITH BBQ ALMONDS

Serves 2

DRESSING

½ cup (75 g) cashews

1 cup (235 ml) water

1 tsp chia seeds

3 tbsp fresh lemon juice

1 tbsp raw apple cider vinegar

1 tbsp cold-pressed extra virgin
   olive oil

1 tbsp miso of your choice

1 tbsp Homemade Mustard (page 135)

1 tsp garlic powder

1 tsp onion powder

1 tbsp mixed Italian dried herbs
   (oregano, basil, dill)

NOODLES

1 large carrot, thin spirals

1 cup (70 g) finely shredded red cabbage
   (use spiralizer to shred)

⅓ medium red onion, finely sliced

1 large handful finely chopped
   mustard greens

1 large button mushroom, thinly sliced

⅓ yellow bell pepper (capsicum),
   finely diced

TOPPINGS

1 handful fresh dill

2–3 large handfuls BBQ Almonds
   (page 148)

1 Add all dressing ingredients to a blender and process until smooth. Transfer the dressing to a large bowl.

2 Add all noodle ingredients to the dressing and toss until thoroughly coated.

3 Top with fresh dill and BBQ Almonds, and serve.

APPLE NOODLE SALAD WITH CABBAGE, DILL, AND MISO MAYO

Serves 1–2

PICKLED ONION
1 red onion, finely sliced

2 tbsp raw apple cider vinegar

1 tbsp maple syrup

MAYO
2 tbsp cashew butter

1 tsp white miso paste

2 tbsp water

1 tbsp raw mustard

3 tbsp raw apple cider vinegar

1 tbsp cold-pressed extra virgin olive oil

1 tbsp cold-pressed walnut oil (you can substitute with olive oil)

NOODLES
½ medium celeriac, thick spirals

2 medium, seasonal apples (Pink Ladies are nice), thick spirals

3 tbsp fresh lemon juice

3 tbsp water

1 tbsp ground dried inca berries

2 large handfuls finely shredded red cabbage (use spiralizer to shred)

½ handful fresh dill

¼ tsp freshly cracked black pepper

¼ tsp fennel seeds, ground in a mortar and pestle

TOPPINGS
Smoked Pecans (page 144), to taste

1 Add the red onion, apple cider vinegar, and maple syrup to a large bowl and massage for about 30 seconds. Set aside for 5 minutes to allow the onion to slightly pickle.

2 Place all mayo ingredients in a medium bowl and whisk until combined. Set aside.

3 Place celeriac and apple noodles, lemon juice, and water in a large bowl. Toss to coat the noodles to prevent browning.

4 Add mayo to the bowl with the red onions.

5 Drain the noodles and add to the bowl with the red onions, along with the inca berries, cabbage, dill, black pepper, and fennel seeds.

6 Toss until all ingredients are thoroughly coated in the miso mayo.

7 Top with smoked pecans and serve.

"BACON," LETTUCE, AND TOMATO NOODLES

Serves 2

KALE

2 small handfuls finely shredded kale

5 tablespoons Garlic and Chives Cream
Cheese (page 150)

NOODLES

1 medium zucchini, thin spirals

2 small handfuls chopped iceberg,
romaine, or butter lettuce

TOPPINGS

5–6 cherry tomatoes, quartered

1 large handful Coconut Bacon
(page 143)

1 small handful sunflower sprouts

½ avocado, sliced

Chives, finely chopped, to taste

2 lemon wedges (optional)

1 Place the kale and garlic and chives cream cheese
in a large bowl and massage for a few seconds.

2 Add the zucchini noodles and lettuce to the bowl
and toss until thoroughly coated.

3 Add the toppings and serve with lemon wedges.

BEET, CARROT, AND CABBAGE SALAD WITH GOJI MISO DRESSING

Serves 2

DRESSING

½ cup (125 g) white miso paste

½ cup (120 ml) water

2 tbsp cold-pressed extra virgin olive oil

1 tbsp maple syrup

1 small handful goji berries

1 tbsp raw apple cider vinegar

½ tsp cold-pressed sesame oil

NOODLES

2 medium beets, thin spirals

2 medium carrots, thin spirals

¼ small red cabbage, shredded with spiralizer

1 orange, peeled, seeded, and cubed

1 green (spring) onion, thinly sliced

TOPPINGS

1 small handful cilantro (coriander) leaves

2 tbsp pepitas

2 tbsp sunflower seeds

1   Place all dressing ingredients in a blender and process until smooth and creamy. Transfer to a large bowl.

2   Add all noodle ingredients to the bowl with the dressing and toss until thoroughly coated.

3   Top with cilantro, pepitas, and sunflower seeds, and serve.

THAI-INSPIRED CARROT NOODLES WITH
GINGER-LIME COCONUT DRESSING

Serves 2 (as a light meal)

NOODLES

2 large carrots, thin spirals (I used
   1 purple and 1 yellow carrot)

1 carrot core (left over after spiralizing),
   thinly sliced

1 kale leaf, roughly torn

1 small handful mint leaves

GINGER-LIME-COCONUT
DRESSING

½ cup (120 ml) Coconut Milk
   (page 133) or store-bought
   organic coconut milk

¾-inch (2 cm) piece ginger

1 medium garlic clove

1 tbsp tamari

1 tbsp cold-pressed sesame oil

Juice and zest of ½ lime

1 tsp raw honey or maple syrup

Chili flakes, to taste

1 tsp chia seeds

TOPPINGS

1 tbsp white and/or black sesame seeds

2 lime wedges

1 Place all noodle ingredients in a large bowl.
Set aside.

2 Place all dressing ingredients in a blender and
process until smooth.

3 Add the dressing to the noodles and toss and gently
massage until thoroughly coated and softened.

4 Top with sesame seeds, garnish with lime wedges,
and serve.

ZUCCHINI NOODLES WITH KALE PESTO

Serves 2 (as a light meal)

MARINATED SPROUTS
1 small handful broccoli sprouts
1 tsp raw apple cider vinegar
½ tsp raw honey or maple syrup

PESTO
2 kale leaves, roughly chopped
1 large handful basil leaves
1 cup (142 g) almonds
⅓ cup (45 g) pine nuts
⅓ cup (80 ml) cold-pressed
    extra virgin olive oil
2 small garlic cloves
5–7 tbsp fresh lemon juice
2 tbsp raw apple cider vinegar
¼ cup (48 g) nutritional yeast flakes
1 tsp sea salt flakes
½ tsp freshly cracked black pepper
1 pinch chili flakes

NOODLES
1 medium zucchini, thin spirals

TOPPINGS
2 tbsp crushed almonds
2 tsp white and/or black sesame seeds
2 tsp Turmeric Dukkah (page 141)
2 lemon wedges

1   Place all marinated sprouts ingredients in a large bowl. Massage the sprouts, then set aside for 5–10 minutes to marinate.

2   Place all pesto ingredients in a food processor and blend until creamy but still chunky.

3   Add 1 cup (260 g) pesto to the bowl with the sprouts. Store the rest in an airtight jar in the refrigerator for up to 5 days.

4   Add the noodles to the bowl with the pesto and toss until thoroughly coated.

5   Top with crushed almonds, sesame seeds, turmeric dukkah, and lemon. Serve immediately.

BEET AND HERB NOODLES WITH PRESERVED LEMON

Serves 2

NOODLES

1 large beet, thin spirals

DRESSING

¼ cup (60 ml) cold-pressed extra
   virgin olive oil

3 tbsp fresh lemon juice

Zest of ½ lemon

1 pinch freshly cracked black pepper

1 pinch chili flakes

SERVING/TOPPINGS

1 small handful roughly chopped
   parsley, divided

1 small handful roughly chopped
   basil, divided

1 small handful roughly chopped cilantro
   (coriander), divided

¼ cup (35 g) almonds

3 tbsp pepitas

2 tbsp pine nuts

1 slice Preserved Lemon (page 146),
   rind and flesh, finely chopped

1   Place beet noodles in a large bowl.

2   Place all dressing ingredients in a small jar, tightly
    seal it with a lid, and shake well until the dressing
    becomes creamy.

3   Add dressing to the noodles and toss until
    thoroughly coated.

4   Place ½ handful each of parsley, basil, and cilantro
    on a platter and arrange noodles on top.

5   Top with the remaining herbs, crushed almonds,
    pepitas, pine nuts, seeds, and preserved lemon,
    and serve.

RAW ZUCCHINI MARINARA

Serves 2–4

SAUCE

1 medium-to-large tomato, roughly
  chopped

½ medium red bell pepper (capsicum),
  roughly chopped

1 small handful basil leaves

2 tbsp cold-pressed extra virgin olive oil

1 tbsp raw honey or maple syrup

1 medium garlic clove, grated

½ tsp garlic powder

⅓ tsp onion powder

½ tsp dried basil

½ tsp dried oregano

⅓ tsp sea salt flakes

¼ tsp freshly cracked black pepper

1 pinch chili flakes or chili powder

1 tbsp chia seeds

1 tbsp linseed meal

NOODLES

1 medium-to-large zucchini, thin spirals

TOPPINGS

5–6 fresh cherry tomatoes

5–6 Dried Tomatoes (page 151)

1 large handful spinach leaves

2 tbsp Raw Parmesan (page 149)

2 tsp nutritional yeast flakes

1 small handful pine nuts, toasted
  (page 131) or raw

1 Except for the chia seeds and linseed meal, add the ingredients for the marinara sauce to a food processor and blend until a chunky mix remains.

2 Transfer marinara sauce to a large bowl, draining the excess juices.

3 Mix in the chia seeds and linseed meal and set sauce aside for 15 minutes.

4 When ready to serve, add the zucchini noodles to the marinara sauce and toss until thoroughly coated.

5 Add toppings and serve immediately.

FOUR NOODLES SUPER BOWL

Serves 1

DRESSING

Juice of 1 lime

1 tbsp white miso paste

1 tbsp cold-pressed extra virgin olive oil

1 tsp cold-pressed sesame oil

1 tsp tamari

1 tsp grated ginger

Freshly cracked black pepper, to taste

Chili flakes, to taste

TOASTED PEANUTS

1 small handful peanuts

1 pinch sea salt flakes

½ tsp paprika

NOODLES

2 large handfuls kelp noodles

¼ medium zucchini, thin spirals

⅓ medium orange carrot, thin spirals

⅓ medium purple carrot, thin spirals

1 large handful chopped kale leaves

1 small handful chopped Thai basil leaves

⅓ medium red bell pepper (capsicum), finely diced

1 green (spring) onion, thinly sliced

4–5 garlic chives, finely chopped

TOPPINGS

2 tbsp white and/or black sesame seeds, lightly toasted (page 131) or raw

2 tbsp hemp hearts

1 Place all dressing ingredients in a large bowl and whisk until combined well. Set aside.

2 Place the peanuts in a small saucepan over low heat. Add sea salt flakes and paprika. Stir often to make sure the peanuts don't burn. They should be lightly toasted after about 3 minutes. Transfer peanuts to a chilled bowl. Set aside.

3 Tear the kelp noodles into smaller pieces and add them to the dressing. Add the rest of the noodle ingredients to the dressing and toss until thoroughly coated.

4 Top with toasted peanuts, sesame seeds, and hemp hearts, and serve immediately.

TURNIP NOODLES WITH ZA'ATAR, PRESERVED LEMON, AND "YOGURT" DRESSING

Serves 2

MARINATED ONIONS

¼ red onion, finely sliced

1 tbsp lemon juice

1 tbsp raw apple cider vinegar

1 tsp maple syrup

DRESSING

1 large handful cashews

1 medium garlic clove

½ tsp garlic powder

½ tsp cumin seeds

½ tsp ground cardamom

2 tbsp cold-pressed extra virgin olive oil

2 tbsp raw apple cider vinegar

2 tbsp fresh lemon juice

⅓ cup (80 ml) water

1 tbsp Za'atar (page 156)

NOODLES

½ medium turnip, thin spirals

1 medium carrot, thin spirals

1 small handful chopped green olives

2 slices Preserved Lemon (page 146), both rind and flesh, finely chopped

TOPPINGS

Fresh cilantro (coriander), to taste

1 sprinkle Za'atar (page 156)

2 tbsp chopped olives of your choice

1 tbsp white and/or black sesame seeds, lightly toasted (page 131)

1 Add the red onion, lemon juice, apple cider vinegar, and maple syrup to a small bowl and massage for 30 seconds.

2 Arrange the red onion slices on a dehydrator mesh tray and dehydrate at 115°F (46°C) for about 30 minutes, until semi-dry. If you don't have a dehydrator, simply arrange the slices on a baking sheet lined with parchment paper and bake at the lowest oven temperature with the door ajar for a few minutes. Keep an eye on them, as they will be ready in a much shorter period of time than required for dehydration.

3 Except for the za'atar, add all ingredients for the "yogurt" dressing to a blender and process until smooth and creamy.

4 Transfer the dressing to a large bowl and stir in the tablespoon of za'atar.

5 Add all noodle ingredients and the onion to the dressing and toss until thoroughly coated.

6 Add the toppings and serve.

MIXED ROOT VEGETABLES WITH AVOCADO DRESSING

Serves 2

NOODLES

1 medium rutabaga (swede), peeled, thin spirals

1 large turnip, thin spirals

1 medium carrot, thin spirals

3 tbsp fresh lemon juice

2 tbsp water

DRESSING

1 small avocado, halved and pitted

3 tbsp fresh lemon juice

1 tbsp raw apple cider vinegar

1 tbsp raw honey or maple syrup

¼ cup (60 ml) cold-pressed extra virgin olive oil

1 tsp sea salt flakes

1 pinch chili flakes

TOPPINGS

2 tbsp poppy seeds

Parsley leaves, to taste

Spicy Cashews (page 145), to taste

1 Place all noodle ingredients in a large bowl and toss to thoroughly coat.

2 Drain the noodles, arrange them on a dehydrator mesh tray, and dehydrate for 30 minutes at 125°F (52°C). If you don't have a dehydrator, simply arrange the noodles on a baking sheet lined with parchment paper and bake at the lowest oven temperature for 5–10 minutes with the door ajar. Keep an eye on them and stir, if needed, so they don't burn.

3 Add all dressing ingredients to a blender and process until smooth and creamy.

4 Transfer dressing to a large bowl, add the dehydrated noodles, and toss until thoroughly coated.

5 Top with poppy seeds, parsley, and spicy cashews, and serve.

PURPLE CARROT NOODLES WITH
THAI COCONUT SAUCE

Serves 2 (as a light meal)

SAUCE

½ cup (120 ml) coconut milk

¾-inch (2 cm) piece ginger

1 medium clove garlic

1 tbsp tamari

1 tbsp cold-pressed sesame oil

Juice and zest of ½ lime

1 tsp coconut sugar

Chili flakes, to taste

NOODLES

2 large purple carrots, thin spirals

TOPPINGS

1 tbsp white and/or black sesame seeds,
  lightly toasted (page 131) or raw

1 small handful mint leaves

1 Place all sauce ingredients in a blender and process until creamy and smooth.

2 Transfer sauce to a large bowl and add the carrot noodles. Toss noodles in the sauce until thoroughly coated.

3 Top with sesame seeds and mint, and serve.

CARROT NOODLES WITH ZESTY GARLIC SAUCE

Serves 1 (as a light meal)

ZESTY GARLIC SAUCE

1 tbsp unhulled tahini (you can substitute with hulled tahini)

1 tbsp cold-pressed walnut oil (you can substitute with olive oil)

3 tbsp fresh lemon juice

1 tsp tamari

1 tsp grated ginger

1 small garlic clove, grated

NOODLES

1 large carrot, thin spirals

TOPPINGS

1 small handful chopped parsley

1 tbsp white sesame seeds, lightly toasted (page 131) or raw

1 tbsp pine nuts, lightly toasted (page 131) or raw

1 Place all sauce ingredients in a blender and process until creamy and smooth.

2 Transfer sauce to a large bowl and add the carrot noodles. Toss noodles in the sauce until thoroughly coated and gently massage them to soften.

3 Top with the parsley, sesame seeds, and pine nuts, and serve.

MISO KOHLRABI NOODLES WITH COCONUT BACON

Serves 2 as a main dish

SNAP PEAS

1 large handful sugar snap peas, julienned

2 tbsp raw apple cider vinegar

1 tsp coconut sugar

1 pinch sea salt flakes

DRESSING

½ cup cold-pressed extra virgin olive oil

3 tbsp raw apple cider vinegar

Juice of ½ orange

1 heaping tsp white miso paste

2 tbsp hulled tahini

1 medium garlic clove

NOODLES

2 small, young kohlrabi (1 green and
    1 purple), thin spirals

1 small carrot, thin spirals

1 green (spring) onion, finely chopped

TOPPINGS

3–4 cherry tomatoes, quartered

1 handful roughly chopped mixed parsley
    and mint

1 large handful Coconut Bacon (page 143)

Chili flakes, to taste

1 Place all ingredients for the snap peas in a medium bowl and massage for 30 seconds. Set aside.

2 Place all dressing ingredients in a blender and process until smooth and creamy. Transfer to a large bowl.

3 Add the kohlrabi and carrot noodles and green onion to the dressing and toss until thoroughly coated.

4 Top with the sugar snap peas, tomatoes, fresh herbs, coconut bacon, and chili flakes, and serve fresh.

ENTRÉES

Seaweed Noodles with Maple Orange Tempeh 80

Broccoli Soba Noodles with Ginger-Lime Tempeh 82

Caramelized Noodles with Herbed Polenta
and Garlic Hemp Sauce 84

Creamy Mushroom "Béchamel" with Tagliatelle 87

Lemon, Parsley, and Bean Noodle Salad with
Tahini Mustard Dressing 88

Curry-Lime Sweet Potato Noodles 90

Carrot Noodles with Carrot Greens Pesto 91

Carrot and Soba Noodles with Peanut Butter Tahini Dressing 92

To-Go Noodles with Kimchi Dressing 94

Potato Pasta Aglio E Olio 97

Noodle Pizza 98

Rainbow Super Bowl 100

Japanese Sweet Potato Noodles with Two Sauces 102

Zucchini Noodle Salad with Moroccan Chickpeas 104

Crustless Cabbage, Potato, and Mushroom Pie 106

Mexican Black Bean Vermicelli Salad with Avocado Tomato Salsa 108

Spicy Apple, Pear, and Kimchi Salad 109

Cooked Zucchini Marinara 110

SEAWEED NOODLES WITH MAPLE ORANGE TEMPEH

Serves 2

TEMPEH
Juice of 1 orange
2 tbsp tamari
1 tbsp maple syrup
1 tbsp Fermented Hot Chili Sauce
  (page 138)
1 tbsp cold-pressed sesame oil
1 block (8 oz/227 g) organic, non-GMO
  tempeh, cubed

SAUCE
1 tbsp hulled tahini
1 tsp unhulled tahini (you can substitute
  with hulled tahini)
3 tbsp fresh lemon juice
2 tbsp cold-pressed extra virgin olive oil
1 small garlic clove, grated
1 tsp white miso paste
Freshly cracked black pepper, to taste

NOODLES
1 medium beet, thin spirals
1 large carrot, thin spirals
2 large handfuls kelp noodles
1 green (spring) onion, thinly sliced
2 small handfuls dulse flakes

TOPPINGS
2 tbsp white and/or black sesame seeds,
  lightly toasted (page 131) or raw
2 raw nori sheets, finely crumbled

1 Except for the cubed tempeh, place all tempeh ingredients in a small pot over medium-low heat. Once hot, add the tempeh cubes, toss to coat, and bring to a boil.

2 Lower the heat, cover, and simmer for 5–10 minutes, or until the tempeh absorbs all of the liquid. Toss every 2–3 minutes to coat tempeh cubes in the aromatic juices.

3 While the tempeh is cooking, place all sauce ingredients in a small bowl and whisk until smooth and creamy. Set aside.

4 Place all noodle ingredients in a large bowl. Add the sauce to the noodles and toss until thoroughly coated—using your hands works best here.

5 Sprinkle sesame seeds and crumbled nori over the noodles, top with hot tempeh cubes, and serve.

Tip: Serve this dish with the Napa Cabbage Kimchi on page 154.

BROCCOLI SOBA NOODLES WITH GINGER-LIME TEMPEH

Serves 2

BROCCOLI FLORETS

Broccoli florets from 1 broccoli head (reserve stalks for noodles)

Juice of ½ lime

1 tbsp tamari

NOODLES

Broccoli stalks, thin spirals

Juice of 1 lime

2 servings soba noodles, cooked according to package instructions, drained, and rinsed under cold water

½ medium zucchini, thin spirals

1 tbsp cold-pressed extra virgin olive oil

1 green (spring) onion, thinly sliced

1 tbsp grated ginger

2 tbsp white and/or black sesame seeds, lightly toasted (page 131)

1 large handful mixed cilantro (coriander) and mint leaves

SAUCE

1 tbsp tamari

Juice of 1 lime

1 tbsp grated ginger

Chili flakes, to taste

TEMPEH

1 tbsp cold-pressed coconut oil

1 block (8 oz/227 g) organic, non-GMO tempeh, cubed

2 tbsp tamari

Juice of 1 lime or from ½ lemon

1 tbsp coconut nectar or maple syrup

1 tbsp Fermented Hot Chili Sauce (page 138)

1 tbsp cold-pressed sesame oil

1 Place all ingredients for the broccoli florets in a large bowl and massage for a few seconds, then set aside for 10 minutes.

2 In a separate large bowl, massage the broccoli noodles with juice from 1 lime for a few seconds. Set aside for 10 minutes.

3 Add the remaining noodle ingredients and broccoli florets to the broccoli and soba noodles. Toss to combine well.

4 Place all sauce ingredients in a small bowl and whisk well to combine.

5 To make the tempeh, heat the coconut oil in a small saucepan over medium heat. Add the tempeh cubes and sauté for a couple of minutes.

6 Add the remaining tempeh ingredients to the saucepan and toss to coat. Cook for about 5 minutes.

7 Once cooked, remove tempeh cubes from the pan, add to the noodles, and serve immediately with the sauce.

CARAMELIZED NOODLES WITH HERBED POLENTA AND GARLIC HEMP SAUCE

Serves 2

SAUCE
⅔ cup (112 g) hemp hearts
⅓ cup (80 ml) cold-pressed extra
   virgin olive oil
½ cup (120 ml) water
2 medium garlic cloves
½ tsp sea salt flakes
¼ cup (60 ml) fresh lemon juice

NOODLES
1 tbsp nigella seeds
2 tbsp cold-pressed coconut oil
1 large red onion, thick spirals
1 medium sweet potato, thick spirals
1 medium-to-large turnip, peeled,
   thick spirals
1 tbsp blackstrap molasses
1 tbsp balsamic vinegar
1 tsp sherry vinegar
1 tsp sea salt flakes
Chili flakes, to taste

POLENTA
2 cups (475 ml) water
1 pinch sea salt flakes
1 tsp Veggie Stock Powder (page 153)
½ cup (80 g) fine maize (cornmeal)
3 tbsp cold-pressed olive oil
1 large handful chopped parsley

1   Place all ingredients for the garlic hemp sauce in a blender and process until smooth and creamy. Set aside.

2   In a large saucepan over medium heat, toast the nigella seeds for 1–2 minutes, or until fragrant.

3   Add the coconut oil to the saucepan and heat for 1–2 minutes. Add the onion, sweet potato, and turnip noodles to the pan and toss to coat in the coconut oil.

4   Add the molasses, both vinegars, salt, and chili flakes. Cook on medium heat for 5–10 minutes, stirring occasionally, until the noodles caramelize.

5   While the noodles are caramelizing, make the polenta. Place the water, salt, and veggie stock powder in a medium stockpot and bring to a boil.

6   Add the fine maize and stir well. Cook on low heat, stirring continuously, until thickened. Depending on the type of maize used, this can take anywhere from 2–15 minutes.

7   When polenta is ready, stir in olive oil and parsley, and mix thoroughly until creamy.

8   Transfer the polenta to a large serving plate and stack the noodles on top. Drizzle with half of the garlic hemp sauce and serve hot.

Note: The garlic hemp sauce makes double than required for this recipe. Store the remainder in an airtight jar in the refrigerator. It will keep for up to 4–5 days and makes a wonderful addition to salads and sandwiches.

CREAMY MUSHROOM "BÉCHAMEL" WITH TAGLIATELLE

Serves 2 (as a light meal)

SAUCE

2 medium handfuls cashews

1¾ cups (400 ml) Coconut Milk (page 133) or 1 13.5-oz can organic coconut milk

2 tbsp cold-pressed coconut oil

1 medium onion, finely chopped

2 large field mushrooms, roughly chopped

½ cup (120 ml) water

¼ tsp freshly grated nutmeg

1 tsp sea salt flakes

NOODLES

1 medium celeriac, peeled, thick spirals

TOPPINGS

1 large handful roughly chopped parsley or 2 tablespoons finely chopped green (spring) onion

1 fresh chili, finely chopped, to taste

1   To make the "béchamel" sauce, place cashews and coconut milk in a blender and process until very smooth. Set aside.

2   Add coconut oil to a medium saucepan over medium heat. Add onion to saucepan and sauté until translucent.

3   Add mushrooms and continue to cook for another 2 minutes, stirring occasionally.

4   Add the cashew and coconut milk mixture, water, nutmeg, and sea salt to the saucepan. Stir, cover, and cook for 10 minutes. Taste and adjust seasonings as needed.

5   Add celeriac noodles to "béchamel" sauce and toss until thoroughly coated.

6   Transfer noodles to serving bowls, top with parsley or green onion and chili, and serve.

LEMON, PARSLEY, AND BEAN NOODLE SALAD WITH TAHINI MUSTARD DRESSING

Serves 1–2

QUINOA

¼ cup (85 g) quinoa

1 cup (240 ml) water

DRESSING

¼ cup (60 ml) fresh lemon juice

2 tbsp cold-pressed extra virgin olive oil

2 tbsp hulled tahini

1 tsp Homemade Mustard (page 135)

1 tsp garlic powder

⅓ tsp sea salt flakes

NOODLES

½ medium zucchini, thin spirals

½ medium-to-large carrot, thin spirals

1 15-oz (425 g) can organic cooked cannellini beans, drained

2 tbsp currants

1 small handful roughly chopped parsley

1 small handful roughly chopped mint

2 small green (spring) onions, thinly sliced

TOPPINGS

1 small handful mixed parsley and mint leaves

1 Add the uncooked quinoa and water to a medium pot over medium heat and bring to a boil.

2 Lower the heat and continue to simmer the quinoa, covered, until it absorbs the water. Turn off the heat.

3 Place all dressing ingredients in a small bowl and whisk until creamy.

4 Place noodle ingredients in a large bowl, add the dressing, and toss until thoroughly coated.

5 Top with extra herbs and serve.

CURRY-LIME SWEET POTATO NOODLES

Serves 2 (as a light meal)

NOODLES

2 tbsp cold-pressed coconut oil

2 medium sweet potatoes,
   thick spirals

DRESSING

1 tbsp Curry Powder (page 137)

1 medium handful cashews

½ cup (120 ml) water

Juice of ½ lime

1 medium garlic clove

1 tbsp white miso paste

1 tsp garlic powder

1 tsp onion powder

TOPPINGS

2 tbsp Curry Crumble (page 142)

1 small handful cilantro
   (coriander) leaves

2 lime wedges

1 Heat the coconut oil in a medium saucepan over medium heat. Add the sweet potato noodles and cook for 4–5 minutes, or until softened. Transfer noodles to a large bowl.

2 Place all dressing ingredients in a blender and process until mixed but still chunky.

3 Add the dressing to the noodles and toss until thoroughly coated.

4 Add toppings, garnish with lime wedges, and serve warm.

CARROT NOODLES WITH CARROT GREENS PESTO

Serves 2 (as a light meal)

PESTO

1 large handful carrot greens (see Noodles below)

1 large handful basil leaves

1 cup (130 g) almonds

6 tablespoons cold-pressed extra virgin olive oil

2 tbsp raw apple cider vinegar

2 tbsp fresh lemon juice

1 tsp garlic powder

1 small garlic clove, grated

2 tbsp nutritional yeast flakes

1 tsp sea salt flakes

½ tsp freshly cracked black pepper

NOODLES

2 large carrots, thin spirals (reserve carrot greens for pesto)

2 large handfuls cooked edamame beans

TOPPINGS

¼ cup (31 g) Curry Crumble (page 142)

1 Place all ingredients for the pesto in a food processor and blend until creamy but still chunky, stopping and scraping the sides down as necessary.

2 Place the carrot noodles and edamame in a large bowl. Add ¼ cup (65 g) pesto to the noodles and massage until thoroughly coated. Store the leftover pesto sauce in an airtight container in the refrigerator for up to 5 days.

3 Top with curry crumble and serve.

CARROT AND SOBA NOODLES WITH PEANUT BUTTER TAHINI DRESSING

Serves 2

DRESSING

1 heaping tsp hulled tahini

1 heaping tsp peanut butter

⅔ tsp tamari

2 drops cold-pressed sesame oil

¼ tsp coconut sugar

½ tsp grated ginger

1 tsp brine from Sweet-and-Sour Pickled Shiitake (page 152)

¼ cup (60 ml) water

1 tbsp fresh lime juice

NOODLES

1 tbsp cold-pressed coconut oil

2 large carrots, thin spirals

1 large handful Sweet-and-Sour Pickled Shiitake (page 152), sliced

1 slice ginger (from brine of Sweet-and-Sour Pickled Shiitake on page 152)

1 tsp cold-pressed sesame oil

1 tsp tamari

1 tbsp brine from Sweet-and-Sour Pickled Shiitake (page 152)

2 handfuls finely shredded iceberg, romaine, or butter lettuce

½ Lebanese cucumber, thin spirals

1 green (spring) onion, thinly sliced

1 serving soba noodles, cooked according to package instructions, drained, and rinsed under cold water

TOPPINGS

1 tbsp dulse flakes

¼ cup (36 g) white and/or black sesame seeds, lightly toasted (page 131)

1 Add all dressing ingredients to a medium bowl and whisk until creamy. Set aside.

2 Heat the coconut oil in a large wok over medium-high heat. Add the carrot noodles, pickled shiitake, and pickled ginger to the wok and toss. Cook over medium-high heat until softened and slightly caramelized, about 4 minutes.

3 Add the sesame oil, tamari, and tablespoon of brine. Toss to thoroughly coat the carrot noodles.

4 Add the shredded lettuce to the wok and toss to mix. Cook for 1 minute, then remove wok from heat.

5 Add the cucumber noodles, green onion, and soba noodles to the carrot noodle mixture.

6 Top with peanut butter tahini dressing, dulse flakes, and toasted sesame seeds, and serve.

TO-GO NOODLES WITH KIMCHI DRESSING

Serves 1 (as a light meal)

QUINOA
½ cup (85 g) red quinoa

1 cup (240 ml) water

DRESSING
2 tbsp Garlic and Chives Cream
  Cheese (page 150)

¼ cup (60 ml) kimchi liquid from
  Napa Cabbage Kimchi (page 154)

NOODLES
1 medium handful finely chopped
  iceberg lettuce

¼ medium zucchini, thick spirals

½ medium sweet dumpling squash,
  thick spirals

2 tbsp raw sunflower seeds

TOPPINGS
4–5 sunflower sprouts

2–3 parsley leaves

1   Add the uncooked quinoa and water to a medium
    pot over medium heat and bring to a boil.

2   Lower the heat and continue to simmer the
    quinoa, covered, until it absorbs the water. Turn
    off the heat.

3   Place all dressing ingredients in a small bowl and
    mix until smooth and creamy. Pour dressing into
    the bottom of a 16-oz (500 ml) jar.

4   Place the lettuce on top of the dressing—the crisp
    lettuce will create a barrier, sealing the dressing
    from the rest of the ingredients.

5   Top lettuce with zucchini and squash noodles, then
    layer on the quinoa and sunflower seeds.

6   Top with the sprouts and parsley.

7   When ready to eat, shake the jar well to thoroughly
    coat all ingredients in the dressing.

POTATO PASTA AGLIO E OLIO

Serves 2

NOODLES

5 medium russet potatoes, thin spirals

1 medium white sweet potato,
   thin spirals

½ medium daikon radish, thin spirals

SAUCE

1 tbsp cold-pressed coconut oil

1 pinch dried rosemary

1 pinch dried basil

1 pinch dried parsley

½ medium red onion, thinly sliced

1 tsp chili flakes

4 medium garlic cloves, thinly sliced

1 small handful currants

1 tbsp raw apple cider vinegar

1 tsp paprika

1 tsp ground turmeric

TOPPINGS

1 tsp Turmeric Dukkah (page 141)
   or Curry Crumble (page 142)

1 tbsp hemp hearts

1 small handful parsley leaves

1 small handful dill

1 Fill a large pot with water and bring to a boil. Add potato noodles and boil for approximately 1 minute. Drain and set aside.

2 Repeat step 1 for the white sweet potato noodles.

3 To make the sauce, heat coconut oil in a medium saucepan over medium heat, then add the rosemary, basil, and parsley. Cook for 1 minute.

4 Add the onion and chili flakes to the pan and continue to cook for 5 minutes, stirring occasionally to prevent the onion from sticking and ensuring even cooking.

5 Add the garlic and currants to the pan and cook for another 5 minutes, stirring occasionally.

6 Add the apple cider vinegar and stir.

7 Add the russet potato noodles and mix. Cook with the lid on for 5–10 minutes, until noodles are almost tender.

8 Slowly stir in the paprika and turmeric, then add the sweet potato noodles to the pan on top of the russet potato noodles and cook for another couple of minutes with the lid on until noodles are tender enough to eat.

9 Remove pan from heat and serve noodles warm topped with turmeric dukkah or curry crumble, hemp hearts, and parsley and dill.

NOODLE PIZZA

Serves 2

CRUST

1 15.5-oz (439 g) can organic cooked
  chickpeas, drained

½ cup (120 ml) water

1 tsp cumin powder

½ tsp paprika

1 pinch sea salt flakes

¼ medium zucchini, diced

⅓ cup (56 g) hemp hearts

SAUCE

½ large red bell pepper (capsicum),
  roughly chopped

NOODLES

½ medium zucchini, ribbon spirals
  (spiralize on the flat blade)

½ medium sweet potato, thick spirals

TOPPINGS

1 small baby eggplant, thinly sliced

1 medium button mushroom, thinly sliced

Garlic and Chives Cream Cheese
  (page 150), to taste

1 tsp onion flakes

Basil leaves, to taste

Fermented Hot Chili Sauce (page 138),
  to taste

1 Preheat oven to 375°F (190°C).

2 Except for the hemp hearts, place all crust
   ingredients in a food processor and blend until
   smooth but still slightly chunky.

3 Transfer crust mixture to a medium bowl and fold
   in the hemp hearts.

4 Spread the crust onto a large baking pan lined
   with parchment paper, about ½ inch (1.5 cm) thick.

5 Bake crust for 20–25 minutes, checking it after
   10–15 minutes to make sure it isn't burning.

6 While baking the crust, place the red pepper in a
   blender and purée. Set aside.

7 Remove the crust from the oven and allow to
   cool in the pan for at least 10–15 minutes or until
   completely cooled.

8 Spread half of the red pepper sauce onto the pizza
   crust, then distribute the zucchini ribbons, sweet
   potato noodles, eggplant, and mushrooms. Add the
   remaining red pepper sauce and top with dollops
   of cream cheese and the onion flakes.

9 Place the pizza back in the oven and bake for an
   additional 15 minutes, or until the toppings are
   tender but still crunchy.

10 Top with fresh basil and chili sauce, and serve.

RAINBOW SUPER BOWL

Serves 2

TEMPEH

½ block (4 oz/114 g) organic,
non-GMO tempeh

DRESSING

1 green (spring) onion, roughly chopped

¾-inch (2 cm) piece ginger

1 small handful parsley stalks

2 tbsp kimchi liquid from Napa
Cabbage Kimchi (page 154)

1 tbsp Napa Cabbage Kimchi (page 154)

2 tbsp hulled tahini

1 small garlic clove

2 tbsp cold-pressed extra virgin
olive oil

2 tbsp raw apple cider vinegar

¼ cup (42 g) hemp hearts

1 small handful cashews

NOODLES

⅓ medium yellow squash,
thin spirals

2 medium carrots, thin spirals

1 large beet, thin spirals

1 cup (155 g) cooked
edamame beans

⅔ cup (55 g) sprouted (or
cooked) wild rice

½ cup (35 g) Napa Cabbage
Kimchi (page 154)

TOPPINGS

2 small handfuls sunflower
sprouts

2 tbsp white and/or black
sesame seeds, lightly toasted
(page 131)

2 lemon wedges

1 Slice the tempeh horizontally into 2 thinner slices, then cut each slice into 2 triangles
for a total of 4 thin tempeh triangles.

2 Heat a medium grill pan over medium heat. Add the tempeh and cook each side for
4–5 minutes. Remove tempeh from the pan and set aside to cool for 5–10 minutes.

3 Place all dressing ingredients in a blender and process until smooth. Set aside.

4 To build your super bowls, arrange all of the components next to each other in
the serving bowls: the 3 types of noodles, wild rice, edamame, kimchi, and tempeh.
Scoop the dressing in the middle of the bowls, then top with the sprouts and
sesame seeds.

5 Serve fresh with lemon wedges.

Sprouting Wild Rice

To sprout rice and enjoy it completely raw and full of goodness, rinse well, place in a bowl, and cover with water. Cover the bowl with a lid or cling wrap and refrigerate.

Drain and rinse the rice twice a day—in the morning and in the evening—for 3–4 days, until you see it "blooming" (some of the seeds will split open). Taste the rice and if it is tender enough to eat, it is ready. Rinse and store in the refrigerator, in an airtight container, for up to 3 days.

JAPANESE SWEET POTATO NOODLES WITH TWO SAUCES

Serves 2

SOUR PLUM SAUCE
2 umeboshi plums, mashed or 1 tbsp
    umeboshi paste
1 tsp white miso paste
2 tbsp maple syrup
1 tsp water
1 tsp cold-pressed sesame oil
1 tbsp pomegranate molasses
1 tbsp mirin
1 tsp Homemade Mustard (page 135)
2 tbsp orange juice

SESAME YUZU SAUCE
2 tbsp hulled tahini
¼ cup (60 ml) yuzu juice (you can
    substitute lime juice)
2 tbsp raw apple cider vinegar
¼ cup (60 ml) cold-pressed extra
    virgin olive oil
2 tsp cold-pressed sesame oil

NOODLES
1 tbsp brown rice oil or cold-pressed
    coconut oil
1 large sweet potato, thick spirals
½ tsp cold-pressed sesame oil
2 tbsp tamari
3 tbsp fresh lemon juice
2 tbsp sake
1 tbsp water

TOPPINGS
2 tbsp white and/or black sesame
    seeds, lightly toasted (page 131)

1 Place all sour plum sauce ingredients in a blender and process until smooth. Set aside.

2 Place all sesame yuzu sauce ingredients in a small bowl and whisk until smooth and creamy. Set aside.

3 Heat the brown rice oil or coconut oil in a medium saucepan over medium-high heat. Add the sweet potato noodles to the saucepan and cook for 3–4 minutes.

4 Add the sesame oil, tamari, lemon juice, sake, and water to the saucepan, and toss to coat. Place a piece of parchment paper cut to the size of the pan over the noodles to create steam (a lid will not achieve the same effect). Cook for 10–15 minutes, until noodles are tender enough to eat.

5 Arrange noodles on a plate and serve with both sauces.

ZUCCHINI NOODLE SALAD WITH MOROCCAN CHICKPEAS

Serves 2

NOODLES

½ medium zucchini, ribbon spirals
  (spiralize on the flat blade)
¼ cup (60 ml) fresh lemon juice
1 pinch sea salt flakes

CHICKPEAS

2 tbsp chopped red onions
1 tsp raw apple cider vinegar
½ tsp coconut nectar or maple syrup
1 15.5-oz (439 g) can organic cooked
  chickpeas, drained
½ medium carrot, grated
1 small handful chopped mint leaves
3 tbsp currants

DRESSING

1 tsp cumin seeds, roughly ground
  with a mortar and pestle
¼ cup (60 ml) cold-pressed extra
  virgin olive oil
2 tsp hulled tahini
1 tbsp raw apple cider vinegar
⅓ tsp garlic powder
⅓ tsp onion powder
⅓ tsp sea salt flakes

TOPPINGS

2 lemon wedges, peeled and seeded
1 small handful parsley leaves
2 tbsp white and/or black sesame seeds,
  lightly toasted (page 131)

1 Place all noodle ingredients in a medium bowl and gently massage for 30 seconds. Set aside.

2 To make the Moroccan chickpeas, place the red onion in a medium bowl with the apple cider vinegar and the coconut nectar, and mix well. Set aside for 2 minutes.

3 Add the chickpeas, carrot, mint, and currants to the onion, and combine.

4 Place all dressing ingredients in a small bowl and whisk until creamy.

5 Add the dressing to the chickpea mixture and toss until thoroughly coated.

6 Divide and arrange zucchini noodles on serving plates, spoon the chickpeas on top, add toppings, and serve.

CRUSTLESS CABBAGE, POTATO, AND MUSHROOM PIE

Serves 4 (makes one 7½-inch/19-cm pie)

FILLING

5 whole cabbage leaves (from the outside layers)

2 medium russet potatoes, peeled and roughly chopped

2 tbsp cold-pressed coconut oil, divided

½ large red onion, finely chopped

1 green (spring) onion, thinly sliced

NOODLES

1 small sweet potato, thin spirals

¼ medium zucchini, thick spirals (cut spirals into smaller pieces)

½ medium green cabbage, shredded with spiralizer

1 tsp sea salt flakes

½ tsp freshly cracked black pepper, plus extra, to taste

3 button mushrooms, thinly sliced

Chili flakes, to taste

1 tbsp raw apple cider vinegar

1 tsp mixed dried Italian herbs (parsley, basil, oregano)

1 Bring a large pot of water to boil and add whole cabbage leaves. Lower heat and simmer 2–3 minutes, until just softened. Drain and rinse with cold water. Pat dry with a paper towel and set aside.

2 In the same pot, add potatoes and enough water to cover them. Cook over medium heat until tender. Drain and set aside.

3 Preheat the oven to 375°F (190°C) and line a 7½-inch (19 cm) pie pan with parchment paper—just enough to cover the bottom and sides of pan.

4 Heat 1 tablespoon coconut oil in a large saucepan over medium heat. Add red onion and cook for 5 minutes, or until soft and translucent.

5 Add green onion and cook for 2 minutes, stirring occasionally.

6 Add sweet potato and zucchini noodles and shredded cabbage. Cook for 5–7 minutes, stirring occasionally, until the vegetables become tender. Season with sea salt and pepper.

7 While noodles cook, mash potatoes in a large bowl.

8 Add noodle mixture, sliced mushrooms, chili flakes, apple cider vinegar, Italian herbs, and 1 tablespoon coconut oil to mashed potatoes, and combine well.

9   Remove the thick vein from each cabbage leaf, then use 3 leaves to carefully line the pie pan, making sure they cover the bottom and sides.

10 Scoop cabbage potato mixture into the pie pan and press it firmly down. Cover with the remaining 2 cabbage leaves and sprinkle a bit of freshly cracked black pepper on top.

11 Fill a 9 × 9-inch (22 × 22 cm) or larger pan with water, one-third full.

12 Cover pie with parchment paper (make sure to cut to size so no edges fall on the outside of the pan) and place the pie pan in the pan with water.

13 Bake for 40–60 minutes (depending on the type of oven). The pie is ready when most of the moisture from the filling is gone and the cabbage leaves on top are soft and tender.

14 This pie is best enjoyed warm, fresh out of the oven. If serving later, store in the refrigerator for up to 3 days. It may also be served chilled.

MEXICAN BLACK BEAN VERMICELLI SALAD WITH AVOCADO TOMATO SALSA

Serves 2

NOODLES

1 medium-to-large chayote, thin spirals

1½ cups (400 g) organic cooked
  black beans, drained

1 cup (roughly ½ corn cob) cooked
  sweet corn kernels

1 green (spring) onion, thinly sliced

½ medium yellow bell pepper (capsicum),
  diced

1 small orange, peeled, seeded,
  and chopped

1 large handful chopped iceberg,
  romaine, or butter lettuce

1 small handful mint leaves

1 small handful cilantro (coriander) leaves

1 medium garlic clove, grated

3 tbsp cold-pressed extra virgin olive oil

SALSA

1 avocado, halved, pitted, and finely cubed

5–6 cherry tomatoes, roughly chopped

1 fresh chili, thinly sliced (hot or mild as
  you prefer, to taste)

Juice and zest of 1 lime

3 tbsp cold-pressed extra virgin olive oil

⅓ tsp sea salt flakes

1 pinch freshly cracked black pepper

TOPPINGS

Mint leaves, to taste

2 slices avocado

Chili flakes, to taste

1 Place all noodles ingredients in a large bowl and
  toss to combine well.

2 Place all salsa ingredients in a medium bowl
  and mix well.

3 Transfer the salsa to the noodle bowl and toss
  until thoroughly coated.

4 Top with mint, avocado, and chili flakes, and
  serve immediately.

SPICY APPLE, PEAR, AND KIMCHI SALAD

Serves 2

DRESSING

2 tbsp kimchi liquid from Napa
   Cabbage Kimchi (page 154)

1 tbsp tamari

1 tsp grated ginger

1 tsp cold-pressed sesame oil

NOODLES

1 large green apple, thin spirals

1 medium, firm Asian (nashi) pear,
   thin spirals

½ cup (82 g) sprouted (or cooked)
   wild rice (see Sprouting Wild Rice
   on page 101)

½ cup (78 g) cooked edamame beans

1 small handful finely chopped green
   (spring) onion (green part only)

3 tbsp Napa Cabbage Kimchi
   (page 154)

TOPPINGS

2 tsp dulse flakes

1   Place all dressing ingredients in a large bowl
    and whisk to combine.

2   Add all noodle ingredients to the dressing and
    toss thoroughly until coated.

3   Top with dulse flakes and serve.

COOKED ZUCCHINI MARINARA

Serves 2

SAUCE

3 tbsp cold-pressed extra virgin olive oil

1 medium red onion, finely chopped

1 medium carrot, diced

1 medium celery rib, diced

1 small handful currants

1 pinch sea salt flakes

1 pinch freshly cracked black pepper

1 tsp fennel seeds

1 28-oz (794 g) can organic whole
    peeled tomatoes

2 tbsp water

Chili flakes, to taste

1 bay leaf

6 medium garlic cloves, thinly sliced

1 pinch saffron threads

NOODLES

1 medium zucchini, thin spirals

TOPPINGS

Raw Parmesan (page 149), to taste

Fresh herbs (parsley, basil), to taste

1   Heat the olive oil in a medium saucepan over medium-low heat. Add the onion and cook for a few minutes, until translucent, being careful not to burn it. (Cooking the onion on low heat will help release more of its sweetness.)

2   Add the carrot, celery, and currants to the pan. Stir, cover the pan, and cook for 3 minutes.

3   Remove the lid, add the sea salt, black pepper, and fennel seeds, and stir again.

4   Roughly squash the tomatoes and add them to the pan, along with the water, chili flakes, and bay leaf. Stir in the garlic and saffron.

5   Let the sauce simmer on medium-low heat for roughly 15 minutes, or until it reaches the desired consistency.

6   Mix in the zucchini noodles, add the toppings, and serve warm.

DESSERTS

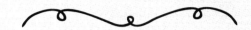

Coconut Cinnamon Carrot Cakes 114

Butternut Squash Pancakes 116

Carrot Cake Noodles 119

Coconut Sugar Apple Pie with
Blueberry Jam and Vanilla Nice Cream 120

Butternut Squash Noodle Balls 122

Pear Noodles with Chocolate Sauce 124

Sweet Potato Brownies 126

Coconut Water Ice Pops 128

COCONUT CINNAMON CARROT CAKES

Makes 4 cakes

NOODLES

2 medium-to-large carrots, thick spirals

2 tbsp melted cold-pressed coconut oil

10 tbsp (44 g) desiccated coconut, divided

1 tsp ground cinnamon

1 tbsp coconut sugar

1 tbsp coconut nectar, maple syrup, or blackstrap molasses

QUICK CHOCOLATE SAUCE

3 tbsp melted cold-pressed coconut oil

1½ tbsp cacao powder

1 tsp maple syrup or raw honey (optional)

TOPPINGS

Desiccated coconut, to taste

Coconut ice cream or Two-Ingredient Nice Cream (page 157), to taste

1 Preheat oven to 350°F (180°C).

2 Place the carrot noodles in a large bowl and toss with the coconut oil. Add 9 tablespoons (42 g) desiccated coconut, cinnamon, coconut sugar, and coconut nectar to the bowl and massage well to thoroughly coat.

3 Arrange the noodles into 4 equal stacks, about 1 inch (2.5 cm) thick, on a baking sheet lined with parchment paper. Sprinkle the remaining desiccated coconut on top of the cakes.

4 Bake for 10–15 minutes, until golden brown and slightly crispy on top.

5 In the meantime, place all chocolate sauce ingredients in a small bowl and whisk until there are no lumps of cacao powder.

6 Serve the carrot cakes warm, topped with desiccated coconut, a dollop of coconut ice cream or nice cream, and a drizzle of chocolate sauce.

BUTTERNUT SQUASH PANCAKES

Serves 2

NOODLES

¼ medium butternut squash,
    thick spirals

3 tbsp maple syrup

1 tbsp coconut sugar

1 tsp ground cinnamon

⅓ tsp ground ginger

¼ tsp ground nutmeg

1 pinch ground cloves

1 pinch allspice

2 tbsp coconut butter (you can substitute
    with Nut Butter on page 134)

TOPPINGS

Maple syrup, to taste

1 large handful chopped mixed
    walnuts and pecans

1 large handful fresh raspberries

Ground cinnamon, for dusting

1   Place all noodle ingredients in a large bowl and massage to combine well.

2   Divide the noodle mixture into 2 equal portions.

3   Arrange each portion on a dehydrator silicone sheet in the shape of a pancake, approximately 1 inch (2.5 cm) thick. The noodle stack needs to be thick and tightly arranged so that when it dries, it sticks together as a pancake.

4   Dehydrate at 125°F (52°C) for 1 hour, then remove the silicone sheet, carefully transfer pancakes to a dehydrator mesh tray, lower the heat, and continue to dehydrate at 115°F (46°C) for about 4 hours, or until crispy on top.

5   Add toppings and serve immediately.

CARROT CAKE NOODLES

Serves 4

CRUMBLE

¼ cup (8 g) almonds

¼ cup (18 g) coconut chips

¼ tsp ground cinnamon

½ cup (88 g) dates, pitted and packed

½ large carrot, roughly chopped

1 tsp maple syrup

1 tbsp cold-pressed coconut oil

NOODLES

2 medium-to-large carrots, thin spirals

1 tsp raw honey or maple syrup

Juice of ½ mandarin

⅓ tsp ground cinnamon

SAUCE

½ cup (75 g) cashews

1 tsp fresh lemon juice

1 tbsp cold-pressed coconut oil

1 tbsp raw honey or maple syrup

3–4 tbsp water, plus more, if needed, to blend

TOPPINGS

8 fresh mandarin slices, peeled and seeded

1 small handful crumbled pecans

2 tbsp pistachios

1 pinch rose petals

1 Add all ingredients for the crumble to a food processor and blend until crumbly and sticky.

2 Spread the crumble mixture onto a dehydrator mesh tray. Dehydrate at 125°F (52°C) for 1 hour, then lower the heat to 115°F (46°C) for another hour, or until crisp.

3 While dehydrating, place all noodle ingredients in a large bowl. Massage for 1 minute, then set aside for 5 minutes.

4 Add all ingredients for the cream cheese sauce to a blender and process until smooth.

5 Add a heaping tablespoon of cream cheese sauce to a serving plate and spread it onto one-third of the plate. Add a quarter of the noodles on top of the cream cheese sauce and arrange 2 mandarin slices on the side. Top with a quarter of the crumbled pecans, pistachios, and rose petals.

6 Repeat step 5 for the remaining servings.

7 Serve immediately.

COCONUT SUGAR APPLE PIE WITH BLUEBERRY JAM AND VANILLA NICE CREAM

Serves 8–10 (makes one 7½-inch/19-cm pie)

CRUST

1 cup (140 g) almonds

1 cup (100 g) coconut flakes or desiccated coconut

7 large Medjool dates, pitted

NOODLES

2 red apples (pink ladies are beautiful for this), thick spirals

Juice of 1 orange

1 tsp ground cinnamon

¼ cup (55 g) coconut butter

3 tbsp coconut sugar, divided

BLUEBERRY JAM

1 cup (145 g) blueberries

½ tsp ground cinnamon

1½ tbsp chia seeds

VANILLA NICE CREAM

1 pinch vanilla bean seeds

Two Ingredient Nice Cream (page 157)

Ground cinnamon, for dusting

1 To make the crust, place almonds and coconut in a food processor and blend until crumbled. Continue to process and add the dates, one at a time, until the dough becomes sticky.

2 Press the dough into a 7½-inch (19 cm) pie pan lined with parchment paper.

3 Place the apple noodles, orange juice, cinnamon, coconut butter, and 2 tablespoons coconut sugar in a large bowl and massage until noodles are thoroughly coated.

4 Spread the apple noodle mixture onto the pie crust and pat it down.

5 Sprinkle the remaining tablespoon of coconut sugar on top of the pie.

6 Dehydrate at 135°F (57°C) for 1½ hours or place in oven on the lowest temperature and bake for 15–20 minutes with the door ajar.

7 To make the jam, place the blueberries in a blender or food processor and blend until puréed.

8 Transfer blueberries to a medium bowl and stir in the cinnamon and chia seeds. Set aside for 30 minutes, or until it thickens.

9 To make the vanilla nice cream, add the vanilla seeds to the two-ingredient nice cream and combine well.

10 When the pie is ready, top with the blueberry jam and nice cream, dust with cinnamon, and serve immediately.

BUTTERNUT SQUASH NOODLE BALLS

Makes 7–8 balls

NOODLES

¼ medium butternut squash,
  thin spirals, roughly chopped

1 pinch saffron

2 tsp rose water

2 tbsp orange juice

1 pinch ground turmeric

Seeds of 5 green cardamom
  pods, finely ground with a
  mortar and pestle

DOUGH

¾ cup (107 g) almonds

½ cup (88 g) dates, pitted and packed

TOPPINGS

1 tsp ground cinnamon, for dusting

1 Except for the cardamom, place all noodle ingredients in a large bowl. Massage noodles for 30 seconds, then let sit for 2–3 minutes.

2 Add the ground cardamom seeds to the noodles.

3 Place the almonds and soft dates in a food processor and pulse until crumbly and sticky. Add this mixture to the noodles.

4 Using wet hands, combine the noodles with the ingredients in the bowl, then form the mixture into 7–8 balls.

5 Arrange balls on a dehydrator mesh tray and dehydrate at 125°F (52°C) for about 1 hour. If you don't have a dehydrator, simply arrange balls on a baking sheet lined with parchment paper and bake at the lowest oven temperature with the door ajar. Keep an eye on them, as they will be ready in less than half the time required for dehydration.

6 Serve warm with a dusting of cinnamon.

PEAR NOODLES WITH CHOCOLATE SAUCE

Serves 2

CHOCOLATE SAUCE

1½ cups (225 g) cashews

1 cup (235 ml) water

3 tbsp raw honey or maple syrup

5 tbsp cacao powder

Seeds of 1 vanilla bean

1 tsp ground cinnamon

1 pinch cayenne pepper

1 pinch sea salt flakes

NOODLES

2 medium, firm, seasonal pears

TOPPINGS

2 tbsp Buckinis (page 140) or
   crushed almonds, divided

2 tsp cacao nibs, divided

1 tsp chia seeds, divided

1 small handful fresh raspberries

1 Add the chocolate sauce ingredients to a blender and process until smooth and creamy. Transfer sauce to a medium bowl and set aside.

2 Slice off tops of pears and set aside.

3 Spiralize pears on the thin blade, leaving about ¾-inch (2 cm) ends (bottoms).

4 Place the pear bottoms on a plate and spoon 1 tablespoon chocolate sauce onto each one. Sprinkle half of the buckinis or crushed almonds, cacao nibs, and chia seeds between the two, then carefully arrange the pear noodles on top.

5 Spoon another tablespoon of chocolate sauce on top of the pear noodles, sprinkle the remaining buckinis or crushed almonds, cacao nibs, and chia seeds between the two, and add the fresh raspberries.

6 Place the pear tops on top and serve immediately.

SWEET POTATO BROWNIES

Makes 16 brownies (makes a 9 × 9-in/22 × 22-cm pan)

NOODLES

½ medium sweet potato, thick spirals

6 tbsp coconut sugar

½ medium sweet potato, thin spirals

1 tbsp coconut nectar, maple syrup,
    or blackstrap molasses

BROWNIES

1 cup (94 g) almond meal

1 cup (92 g) chickpea flour

½ cup (35 g) desiccated coconut

6 tbsp cacao powder

1 pinch sea salt flakes

1 small sweet potato, peeled
    and cubed

2 ripe bananas

10 Medjool dates, pitted

½ cup (120 ml) water

2 tbsp hulled tahini

TOPPINGS

Chocolate sauce (see Coconut
    Cinnamon Carrot Cakes on
    page 114), to taste

1 Preheat oven to 375°F (190°C).

2 Place the thick sweet potato noodles in a large bowl with coconut sugar and massage until thoroughly coated.

3 In a separate large bowl, place the thin sweet potato noodles with the coconut nectar and toss until thoroughly coated.

4 Place the dry brownie ingredients (almond meal, chickpea flour, coconut, cacao, and sea salt) in a large bowl. Combine.

5 Place the sweet potato cubes, bananas, dates, and water in a blender and process to a smooth paste.

6 Pour the mixture from step 5 on top of the dry brownie mixture, then add the tahini to the bowl. Combine well until a sticky, wet dough forms.

7 Add the thin sweet potato noodle mixture to the dough and mix to incorporate.

8 Line a 9 × 9-inch (22 × 22 cm) pan with parchment paper on the bottom and up the sides.

9 Transfer the brownie mixture to the pan lined with parchment paper and press it down.

10 Top the brownie mix with the thick sweet potato noodles and pat down.

11 Bake the brownies for about 20 minutes, or until done—to test if done, poke a skewer through the middle; if it comes out clean, the brownies are cooked.

12 Remove the brownies from the oven and allow them to cool in the pan for at least 30 minutes or until they reach room temperature.

13 Remove brownies from pan and transfer to a wire rack. Let cool for another 10 minutes.

14 Serve the brownies drizzled with chocolate sauce.

COCONUT WATER ICE POPS

Makes 10 small ice pops

ICE POPS

2 cups (475 ml) coconut water

½ large mango, peeled

1 small handful blueberries

NOODLES

1 firm, seasonal apple, thin spirals

1 Place the coconut water and mango in a blender and purée until smooth.

2 Pour the coconut mango mix into ice pop molds.

3 Add apple noodles, a few blueberries, and a popsicle stick (optional) to each mold.

4 Freeze for at least 6 hours or overnight. Serve frozen.

BASICS, CONDIMENTS, TOPPINGS, AND MORE

ACTIVATED NUTS AND SEEDS

Makes 1½–2 cups (200–400 g)

The soaking of nuts and seeds begins the germination process, makes them easier to digest, and increases the nutrients available for our bodies. It is an easy endeavour and something you might want to consider if you are consuming nuts and seeds on a daily basis, especially for those delicious nut milks and chia puddings.

4 cups or 32 oz (1 L) filtered
   water
1 tsp sea salt flakes

1½–2 cups (200–400 g) nuts or seeds (almonds,
   walnuts, cashews, macadamias, pepitas, chia,
   or any nut or seed of your choice)

1   Place the water and sea salt in a large bowl and stir to dissolve the salt. Add the nuts or seeds to the water, stir, and let soak overnight at room temperature or in the refrigerator during the summer.

2   The next day, rinse the nuts or seeds, drain them, and spread them onto a dehydrator mesh tray. Make sure they are evenly spaced out, with minimum overlap.

3   Dehydrate the nuts at 120°F (48°C), until they are completely dry and crunchy. This can take anywhere from 12–24 hours, depending on what nuts and seeds you use. Make sure you check them after 3–4 hours and turn the trays or mix the nuts or seeds so they dry evenly. If you don't have a dehydrator, arrange the nuts or seeds on a baking sheet lined with parchment paper and bake at the lowest oven temperature with the door ajar. Make sure you turn the nuts or seeds every 15 minutes, checking them often so they don't burn, as they will be ready in less than half the time required for dehydration (this will vary depending on your oven).

4   The nuts are ready when fully dry and crunchy. Mold can form if any moisture is left, so don't worry about over-dehydrating them. If using them within a few weeks, store them in an airtight container in a cool, dry space. If you're keeping them for a few months, store them in an airtight container in the refrigerator.

TOASTED NUTS OR SEEDS

Makes 1½–2 cups (200–400 g)

Toasting nuts and seeds is easy and fast to do, especially if you prefer a rich, roasted flavor. Just make sure to toast only the amount you need for the dish, as the nuts and seeds taste best when freshly toasted.

1½–2 cups (200–400 g) nuts or seeds (peanuts, almonds, walnuts, cashews, pistachios, sesame, pepitas, or any nut or seed of your choice)

1 In a small frying pan, lightly toast the nuts or seeds, stirring constantly, until fragrant, about 2–4 minutes.

2 Transfer to a clean, dry bowl and use immediately.

NUT OR SEED MILK

Makes 32 ounces (1 L)

Nut and seed milks are a healthy, inexpensive, delicious, and dairy-free alternative to milk. You can make milks out of pretty much any of your favorite nuts or seeds, and they can be used in raw or baked recipes as an alternative to regular milk.

INGREDIENTS

4 cups or 32 oz (1 L) filtered water

1½–2 cups (200–400 g) nuts or seeds (almonds, walnuts, cashews, macadamias, pepitas, chia, or any nut or seed of your choice)

1 Place the water and nuts or seeds in a blender and process on high speed for 1 minute, or until smooth and creamy.

2 Strain the milk into a large bowl through a nut milk bag. Do not discard the leftover nut milk pulp from making the milk; it is incredibly delicious and nutritious and you can use it to make cookies, crumbles, or granola. If you are not using the nut milk pulp right away, store it in the refrigerator for up to 3 days or in the freezer for a few weeks.

3 Store nut milk in an airtight jug or jar in the refrigerator for up to 5 days.

Tip: Every now and then, I change things up and make a vanilla, chocolate, turmeric, or caramel milk. To do this, I simply add half a vanilla bean, 2 pitted dates, ½-inch (12 mm) piece fresh turmeric root, or 2 tablespoons cacao to the blender with the nuts, process everything together, and then strain as the recipe calls for.

COCONUT MILK

Makes 32 ounces (1 L)

Similar to nut and seed milks, coconut milk is a simple and inexpensive dairy-free milk that you can make at home. You can use it in recipes as you would any other milk or just enjoy it on its own. Below are recipes for making milk with dried and fresh coconut.

DRIED COCONUT

4 cups or 32 oz (1 L) filtered water

2⅓ cups (200 g) dried organic coconut (desiccated or chips)

1 Warm the filtered water in a small saucepan over medium heat. The water should be warm, not hot. Remove from the heat.

2 Add coconut and warm water to a blender and process for 1 minute, until smooth and creamy. Strain the mixture into a large bowl through a nut milk bag.

FRESH COCONUT

1 mature coconut

2 cups or 16 oz (0.5 L) filtered water

1 Crack open the coconut, pour the coconut water into a medium bowl, and scoop out the flesh. Peel and wash the flesh, then add it to a food processor with the coconut water and filtered water.

2 Blend for 2 minutes on high speed, or until creamy and smooth. Strain the coconut milk into a large bowl through a nut milk bag.

Coconut milk is best enjoyed fresh, but it can be stored in an airtight jug or jar in the refrigerator for up to 4 days. If it separates, shake the jar well before use.

Tip: You can flavor coconut milk as you would any Nut or Seed Milk (see opposite page).

NUT BUTTERS

Makes 2 cups (500–600 g)

Nut or seed butters are the answer to many snacking dilemmas. Eat it with sliced fruit, on toasted sourdough, in (and on) cookies, or with and on everything.

You can make nut butter with just a nut or seed or experiment with various combinations of nuts and seeds, cacao, cinnamon, sweetener, dates, and more. You can also lightly toast the nuts and seeds (see page 131) prior to turning them into butter for a roasted, deeper flavor.

INGREDIENTS

4 cups (500–600 g) of your favorite nut or a mix of nuts and/or seeds
½ tsp sea salt flakes

1   Place nuts or seeds in a blender or food processor with the sea salt. If using a larger food processor, add all at once; if using a blender, process in 2 batches.

2   Begin to blend, stopping and scraping down the sides a few times. At first, the nuts and seeds will turn into a fine meal, which will gradually become smoother and runnier. Depending on your appliance and the nut or seed used, it can take anywhere from 1–20 minutes to make nut butter. If your blender or food processor becomes hot at any point, stop blending and allow it to cool before continuing.

3   When it reaches a smooth, creamy consistency, scoop the butter into a jar and store it in an airtight container in the refrigerator. This is best consumed within a couple of weeks, but if stored properly, it keeps for up to a month.

HOMEMADE MUSTARD WITH FRESH HERBS

Makes 1½ cups (375 g)

This mustard packs more flavor, spice, and goodness than any store-bought variety and pairs perfectly with veggie burgers and sandwiches, as well as enhancing a good old-fashioned potato salad and salad dressings.

INGREDIENTS

½ cup (120 ml) raw apple cider vinegar

⅔ cup (160 ml) water, plus additional (2 tbsp at a time), if needed, to blend

⅔ cup (120 g) yellow mustard seeds

2 tbsp fresh thyme

1½ tbsp fresh rosemary

½ tsp chili flakes

⅓ tsp sea salt flakes

1 tsp raw honey or maple syrup

¼ cup (60 ml) water at room temperature

1 Place the apple cider vinegar and water in a medium bowl and add the mustard seeds. Cover and leave to soak for 2–3 days at room temperature or in the refrigerator during the summer—the mustard seeds will absorb almost all of the liquid and start to smell like you're about to make the best mustard on the planet.

2 Place the mustard seed mix in a blender and add the rest of the ingredients. Blend until smooth. If it's too thick, add 2 tablespoons water at a time and continue to blend until smooth.

3 Spoon into airtight jars, leaving no air bubbles, if possible. Cover and refrigerate. The mustard is best when fresh but can be stored in the refrigerator for up to 2–3 months.

HOMEMADE KETCHUP

Makes ¾–1 cup (200–300 g)

This homemade ketchup packs incredible flavor and so many nutritious ingredients. It is mildly hot (something you can adjust to your taste), faintly sweet, and rich. It can be eaten by the spoonful, but it also pairs well in any recipe that calls for chili sauce or ketchup—sandwiches, pasta, sauces, soups, dips, and spreads.

INGREDIENTS

½ cup (about 60 g) tightly packed semi-dried tomatoes (if using store-bought dried tomatoes, soak them in water for 2 hours, then drain and use; if using Dried Tomatoes on page 151, dehydrate for half the time)

2 medium Roma tomatoes, roughly chopped

2 Medjool dates, pitted

1 small garlic clove

5 tbsp cold-pressed extra virgin olive oil

1 tbsp balsamic vinegar

1½ tsp paprika

2 tsp chili flakes

½ tsp dried oregano

½ tsp dried basil

Sea salt flakes, to taste

Freshly cracked black pepper, to taste

1 Place all ingredients in a blender and process until silky smooth with the consistency of ketchup.

2 Spoon into airtight jars, leaving no air bubbles, if possible. Cover and refrigerate. The ketchup is best when fresh but can be stored in the refrigerator for up to 1–2 weeks.

CURRY POWDER

Makes about 1 cup (100 g)

Curry powder is a great spice to have in the pantry and can be used liberally to season a wide range of dishes.

SEEDS

2 tbsp cumin seeds

1 tsp fenugreek seeds

2 tbsp coriander seeds

1 tbsp chili flakes

½ tsp mustard seeds

SPICES

½ tsp sea salt flakes

2 tbsp ground turmeric

1 tbsp freshly cracked black pepper

½ tsp ground ginger

½ tsp ground cinnamon

¼ tsp ground cloves

½ tsp ground cardamom

1   Add all seeds to a mortar and pestle and grind. A rough grind is workable, but a fine powder works best. Pour the ground seeds into a dry, small bowl.

2   Add all spices to the bowl and toss to mix well.

3   Transfer to an airtight jar and store in the pantry. This keeps well for a few months, but it is best to use within a few weeks for maximum flavor.

FERMENTED HOT CHILI SAUCE

Makes 1–1½ cups (250–350 ml)
Cooking time: 4–6 weeks (of waiting)
Special equipment: food scale

This hot chili sauce beats any store-bought version hands down. It is free of additives, preservatives, and artificial colorings, as well as being abundant in probiotic bacteria, which naturally occurs in fermented foods. It is best consumed raw, as heat destroys the good bacteria. It can be used in and on everything that needs a little heat and is guaranteed to become a staple in the pantry of any true chili lover.

INGREDIENTS

14 oz (400 g) fresh chili peppers
  (I used mostly yellow cayenne and
  3–4 bird's eye)
3 medium cloves garlic, finely chopped
Sea salt flakes (see step 2 for amount)
Raw apple cider vinegar (see step 10
  for amount)

1 Cut the stems off the chili peppers. If desired, remove the seeds to reduce their heat.

2 Weigh the chilies with a food scale and calculate 2 percent of this weight, to figure out how much sea salt to add (the recommended amount is 8 grams but you may need more or less depending on your calculation).

3 Roughly chop the peppers and add them to a clean jar (this is the jar in which they will ferment, so it should be large enough to hold the chilies covered in water).

4 Add the garlic, sea salt, and enough water to the jar to cover the chili peppers, plus an extra ¼ inch (6 mm). Make sure all ingredients are submerged.

5 Stir the contents of the jar using a wooden or ceramic spoon, then cover the jar with cheesecloth or a paper towel and secure with an elastic band. Place the jar in a cool, dark place, away from direct sunlight.

6 Check the jar approximately every other day to see if any white mold forms on top. If there is white mold and it doesn't smell bad, simply remove the mold with a clean wooden or ceramic spoon, then rinse the spoon and stir the chili mixture. Re-cover the jar and place it back in the cool, dark place.

7   To make sure that the chilies are fermenting, check for tiny bubbles forming either on top or throughout the chili mixture. Fermentation is complete when these tiny bubbles stop forming. This takes between 4 and 6 weeks, depending on temperature.

8   When fermentation is complete, add the entire mixture to a blender and process until puréed.

9   Strain the purée through a fine sieve and press it with a spoon to get as much juice out as possible. Reserve the juice.

10 Measure the juice from the straining (I had close to 1 cup/220 ml of pure hot liquid gold) and add half of that amount in apple cider vinegar (I added close to ½ cup/110 ml).

11 Place the freshly fermented chili sauce in an airtight jar or bottle and refrigerate. It will be ready to consume the next day, after the flavors have had time to combine. Keep refrigerated until you use up all of the sauce.

Tip: Mix the leftover chili pulp (what is left after straining the juice in step 9) with 2–3 tablespoons olive oil, place it in a small airtight jar, and refrigerate. This by-product is best used within 2–3 weeks and is beautiful when cooked in soups, stews, and other amazing warm meals.

ACTIVATED CRUNCHY BUCKINIS

Makes 1 cup (164 g)

These little seeds of deliciousness are the perfect topping for smoothies, chia puddings, porridges, and even in baked goods like cookies.

1 cup (164 g) raw buckwheat groats

12 cups or 96 oz (3 L) water, divided

2 tbsp maple syrup or raw honey (optional)

2 tsp ground cinnamon (optional)

1 Place buckwheat groats in a large bowl and add 6 cups (1.5 L) water. Stir and let soak overnight at room temperature or in the refrigerator during the summer.

2 The next morning, drain and rinse thoroughly to remove the gooey slime that naturally forms.

3 Soak buckwheat for another 8 hours in another 6 cups (1.5 L) water.

4 Thoroughly drain and rinse buckwheat again.

5 If using the maple syrup or honey, stir it in and toss to coat.

6 Spread buckwheat on dehydrator silicone sheets in a single layer, evenly spaced out and with minimum overlap, and dehydrate at 100°F (42°C) for 12 hours, or until dry and crispy. If you don't have a dehydrator, spread the buckwheat on a baking sheet lined with parchment paper and bake at the lowest oven temperature with the door ajar. Make sure you check it every 10 minutes or so, turning and stirring the buckwheat, so it cooks evenly and doesn't burn. Keep an eye on it as it will be ready in less than half the time required for dehydration (this will vary depending on your oven).

7 Taste and make sure the buckinis are completely dry. Mold can form if any moisture is left.

8 Store the buckinis in an airtight jar in a cool, dry place in the pantry. They will keep well for 4–6 months or longer.

TURMERIC DUKKAH

Makes 2½ cups (350 g)

Dukkah is an Egyptian spice mix made of nuts, seeds, and spices. This homemade version packs plenty of flavor and is perfect sprinkled on fresh salads, roasted vegetables (think sweet potato or pumpkin), dips, soups, or even avocados.

NUTS

1 cup (150 g) almonds

¾ cup (100 g) cashews

⅓ cup (50 g) macadamias

SEEDS AND SPICES

⅓ cup (50 g) white sesame seeds, lightly toasted (page 131)

1 tbsp ground turmeric

1½ tsp cumin seeds

1 tsp whole black peppercorns

⅓ tsp sea salt flakes

½ tsp ground cinnamon

⅓ tsp ground ginger

½ tsp ground coriander

1 pinch chili flakes

1   Place the almonds, cashews, and macadamias in a food processor and blend until crumbled. Transfer the crumbled nuts to a large bowl.

2   Add all seeds and spices ingredients to a mortar and pestle and grind them until fine but still a bit chunky.

3   Add the ground seeds and spices to the bowl with the crumbled nuts and toss to thoroughly mix.

4   Store the dukkah in an airtight jar in the pantry, away from heat and light for up to 2 months. If storing for longer, keep in the refrigerator.

CURRY CRUMBLE

Makes 2 cups (250 g)

This curry crumble builds on the Curry Powder on page 137 and is yet another way of enjoying the wonderful spices that make up a curry flavor in as many dishes as possible.

SPICES

½ tsp ground coriander
¼ tsp ground turmeric
½ tsp cumin seeds
1 pinch ground cardamom
¼ tsp mustard seeds
¼ tsp ground cinnamon
1 pinch chili flakes
1 pinch freshly cracked black pepper
1 pinch sea salt flakes

NUTS

1½ cups (220 g) cashews
½ cup (23 g) sunflower seeds
1 tbsp maple syrup
2 tbsp lime juice

1   Add spices ingredients to a mortar and pestle and grind them until they become a fine powder.

2   Place cashews and sunflower seeds in a food processor with the spice mix, maple syrup, and lime juice, and process until crumbly.

3   Store in an airtight container in the pantry for 2–3 weeks and use as needed.

COCONUT BACON

Makes 1½ cups (180 g)

This vegan version of "bacon" is ridiculously delicious. It's crispy, salty, sweet, smoky, and completely addictive. For extra-crisp texture and "baconish" flavor, the oven method of dehydrating works best.

INGREDIENTS

3 large handfuls coconut chips

3 heaping tbsp organic tomato paste

2 tbsp maple syrup

3 tbsp tamari

1 tbsp liquid smoke (choose a brand that is only made up of smoke and water, with no colorings, artificial flavors, or preservatives; use sparingly)

1 tsp smoked paprika

1 tsp garlic powder

1 Add all ingredients to a large bowl and toss until coconut chips are thoroughly coated.

2 Spread the chips onto a dehydrator mesh tray, in a single layer, evenly spaced out with minimum overlap, and dehydrate at 125°F (52°C) for 1 hour. Lower the temperature to 115°F (46°C) and continue to dehydrate for 4–5 hours, or until fully dry and crispy. If you don't have a dehydrator, spread the coconut chips on a baking sheet lined with parchment paper and bake in the oven at the lowest temperature with the door ajar. Keep an eye on the chips, taking them out and stirring after 15 minutes or so, then every 5–10 minutes, to make sure they don't burn. They will be ready in less than an hour (this can vary depending on your oven).

3 Taste and make sure the coconut chips are completely dry. Mold can form if any moisture is left.

4 Store the coconut chips in a large airtight jar in a cool, dry place in the pantry for up to 2 months.

SMOKED PECANS

Makes 1 cup (150 g)

The wonderful taste of the pecan is made even better when a bit of sweetness, saltiness, and smokiness is added. Plus, they're wonderful for topping salads.

INGREDIENTS

2 large handfuls pecans

1 tbsp liquid smoke or smoked paprika (choose a liquid smoke that is only made up of smoke and water, with nothing else added; use sparingly)

1 tbsp maple syrup

½ tsp sea salt flakes

¼–½ tsp Fermented Hot Chili Sauce (page 138)

1 Place all ingredients in a large bowl and toss until pecans are thoroughly coated.

2 Spread pecans onto a dehydrator mesh tray, in a single layer, evenly spaced out and with minimum overlap, and dehydrate at 115°F (46°C) for approximately 2–3 hours, or until the pecans are no longer wet but still sticky from the syrup. If you don't have a dehydrator, spread the pecans on a baking sheet lined with parchment paper and bake at the lowest oven temperature with the door ajar. Keep an eye on them, stirring every 15 minutes or so, to make sure they dry evenly and don't burn. They will be ready in less than half the time required for dehydration (this will vary depending on your oven).

3 To test if the pecans are fully done, allow them to cool, then taste them. If they are still sticky on the outside, but dry and crispy on the inside, they are done. Mold can form if any moisture is left. Make sure to allow the pecans to cool before using. The longer they sit, the firmer and crunchier they become.

4 Store the pecans in an airtight jar in a cool, dry place in the pantry for up to 2 months.

SPICY CASHEWS

Makes 1 cup (150 g)

Cashews are one of my favorite nuts (though the list is long!), but I often end up enjoying them in sweet recipes. This savory option makes for a wonderful snack and salad- or noodle-topper.

INGREDIENTS
2 large handfuls cashews

½ tsp onion powder

½ tsp smoked paprika

1 tbsp raw apple cider vinegar

1 tbsp Fermented Hot Chili Sauce (page 138)

1 Place all ingredients in a large bowl and toss until the cashews are thoroughly coated.

2 Spread the cashews onto a dehydrator mesh tray, in a single layer, evenly spaced out and with minimum overlap, and dehydrate at 115°F (46°C) for approximately 2–3 hours, or until the cashews are no longer wet. If you don't have a dehydrator, spread the cashews on a baking sheet lined with parchment paper and bake at the lowest oven temperature with the door ajar. Keep an eye on them and stir every 15 minutes or so to make sure they don't burn. They will be ready in less than half the time required for dehydration (this will vary depending on your oven).

3 Taste them to make sure they are completely dry. Mold can form if any moisture is left. Make sure to allow cashews to cool before using. The longer they sit, the firmer and crunchier they become.

4 Store the cashews in an airtight jar in a cool, dry place in the pantry for up to 2 months.

PRESERVED LEMONS

Makes a ½-gallon (2 L) jar
Cooking time: 3–6 weeks (of waiting)

This particular pickle is a Middle Eastern specialty that I fell in love with during my travels through Morocco. When lemons are in season, I preserve enough to last through the year and end up using them in almost everything. They add a depth of flavor when blended into dressings and dips, or finely chopped into healthy grain dishes and salads, or cooked in stews, soups, and couscous dishes.

10–12 medium organic lemons,
  washed well

1 cup (292 g) sea salt flakes, divided

1 cinnamon stick, halved

5 cloves, divided

2 star anise, divided

½ tsp whole black peppercorns, divided

Fresh lemon juice of 4–5 lemons,
  as needed

1 Wash and air-dry a ½-gallon (2 L) glass jar with a plastic or plastic-lined lid. Wash and air-dry lemons to remove any surface dust or dirt. Scrub the lemons, if needed, to remove dirt. Trim both ends of each lemon and cut into thick slices or half slices. You should get between 6–8 slices per lemon

2 Place 1 teaspoon sea salt and half of all spices (cinnamon stick, cloves, star anise, and peppercorns) in the bottom of the clean jar.

3 Arrange a layer of lemon slices and gently press them down. Depending on how wide or narrow your jar is, you should be able to fit 1–4 tightly packed slices into a layer. Then sprinkle approximately 1 teaspoon of salt. Repeat this step.

4 Add the remaining spices halfway through the jar, then repeat step 4 until the jar is almost full, leaving a ¾-inch (2 cm) space.

5 There should already be lemon juice in the jar from pressing down the lemon slices. Add more, as necessary, to completely cover the lemons in juice and fill the jar almost to the top, leaving a little more than ⅓-inch (1 cm) space.

6   Tightly screw lid on the jar and let it sit at room temperature in a cool, dry place, such as a pantry, for about 1 week, tipping the jar once a day and putting it back upright. After 1 week, move the jar to the refrigerator and let it sit for at least 3 weeks, ideally 6 weeks. In the wintertime, you can leave the jar in a cool place in the pantry instead of the refrigerator.

7   When done, store in a cool, dry place. If correctly preserved, lemons will keep, sealed, for 1–2 years. Once opened, keep the jar in the refrigerator and use within 3–4 months.

Tip: Traditionally, lemons are preserved whole or quartered. I find that slicing them allows more lemons to be packed in a jar, saving space in the pantry. Also, traditionally, the flesh is discarded and only the rind is used in recipes; however, I use the whole preserved lemon—flesh and rind—and love them both. Just make sure you remove the pits before using.

BBQ ALMONDS

Makes 1¾ cups (250 g)

This is an all-around delicious recipe that goes with everything. These almonds make for an addictive and nutritious snack, but are also great in salads.

INGREDIENTS

1 medium Roma tomato,
    roughly chopped

3 tbsp tamari

2 tbsp maple syrup

1 heaping tsp smoked paprika

4 large handfuls raw almonds

1 Place the tomato, tamari, maple syrup, and paprika in a food processor and blend until smooth. Transfer mixture to a large bowl.

2 Add the almonds to the bowl and toss until they are thoroughly coated.

3 Spread the almonds onto a dehydrator silicone sheet, in a single layer, evenly spaced out and with minimum overlap, and dehydrate for 1 hour at 125°F (52°C). Lower the heat to 115°F (46°C) and dehydrate for another 2 hours. When the almonds are sticky and there is no more liquid, transfer them to a mesh sheet and continue to dehydrate for another 3 hours, or until completely dry. If you don't have a dehydrator, spread the almonds on a baking sheet lined with parchment paper and bake at the lowest oven temperature with the door ajar. Keep an eye on them, stirring every 20 minutes, to make sure they don't burn. They will be ready in less than half the time required for dehydration (this will vary depending on your oven).

4 Taste them to make sure they are fully dry. Mold can form if any moisture is left. Allow the almonds to cool before using. The longer they sit, the firmer and crunchier they become.

5 Store the almonds in an airtight jar in a cool, dry place in the pantry for up to 2 months.

RAW PARMESAN

Makes 1 cup (100 g)

This dairy-free, salty, cheese-like crumble is delicious crumbled on noodles and pasta, soups, salads, and even sandwiches. It's a wonderful alternative to traditional Parmesan and can be used in any recipe that calls for it.

INGREDIENTS

½ cup (75 g) cashews
½ cup (84 g) hemp hearts
6 tbsp raw apple cider vinegar
1 tbsp white miso paste
1 tsp dried oregano
1 tsp dried basil
3 tbsp nutritional yeast flakes

1 Place the cashews into a food processor and blend until you obtain a fine meal.

2 Transfer cashews to a large bowl with the rest of the ingredients and mix by hand until the mixture resembles a paste.

3 Spread the paste onto a dehydrator silicone sheet in a thin layer (about ¼ inch/6 mm thick), evenly spaced out and with minimum overlap, and dehydrate at 115°F (46°C) for about 3–4 hours, or until crispy. If you don't have a dehydrator, spread the paste on a baking sheet lined with parchment paper and bake at the lowest oven temperature with the door ajar. Keep an eye on it, stirring every 5–10 minutes to make sure it doesn't burn. It will be ready in about 30 minutes, though this time can vary depending on your oven.

4 Taste to make sure the parmesan is fully dry. Mold can form if any moisture is left.

5 Store the parmesan in an airtight container in a cool, dry place in the pantry for up to 1 month.

GARLIC AND CHIVES CREAM CHEESE

Makes 2 cups (500 g)

Whether or not you are dairy intolerant or vegan, this recipe is bound to become a favorite. Tree nut cheeses add a gorgeous creamy texture and flavor to dishes. This soft cream cheese can be used in any recipe that calls for melted cheese, such as to top pizzas or wraps, in dips, or drizzled over stews. This also pairs well on its own with crackers and crudités.

INGREDIENTS

1½ cups (200 g) cashews

2½ tsp cold-pressed extra virgin olive oil

1 cup (235 ml) water

1 tsp garlic powder

3 tbsp fresh lemon juice

1 tsp sea salt flakes

3 tbsp nutritional yeast flakes

1 small handful chopped fresh chives

1   Add the ingredients, except for the chives, to a blender and process into a perfectly smooth cream cheese.

2   Transfer the cheese into a large bowl and fold in the chopped chives.

3   Store in an airtight container in the refrigerator for up to 1 week.

DRIED TOMATOES

Makes 1 cup (54 g)

For this recipe, you can use any tomatoes that are in season but not overripe. Choose ones that are still firm. I love this best with small cherry tomatoes, as they pack so much more flavor and sweetness. The amount of time required to make this recipe varies according to the water content of the tomatoes, the thickness of the slices, and how well the air circulates around them when in the dehydrator/oven.

INGREDIENTS
30 (500 g) cherry tomatoes, halved
3 tbsp cold-pressed extra virgin olive oil
1 tbsp balsamic vinegar
⅓ tsp sea salt flakes
½ tsp dried oregano
½ tsp dried basil
¼ tsp garlic powder

1 Place all ingredients in a medium bowl and toss until tomatoes are thoroughly coated.

2 Arrange the tomatoes in a single layer on a dehydrator mesh tray, skin side down. Doing this preserves the juices inside the tomatoes.

3 Dehydrate at 125°F (52°C) for 2 hours, then lower the temperature to 115°F (46°C) for another 5–6 hours, or until the tomatoes are completely dried. If you don't have a dehydrator, spread the tomatoes, skin side down, on a baking sheet lined with parchment paper and bake at the lowest oven temperature with the door ajar. Keep an eye on them to make sure they don't burn and turn them every now and then to expose all sides.

4 The tomatoes are ready when they are completely dry but not crisp; they should still retain elasticity, but no moisture. Store the tomatoes in an airtight container in the refrigerator for up to 1 month.

SWEET-AND-SOUR PICKLED SHIITAKE

Makes a 1-quart (1 L) jar

These mushrooms are packed with wonderful ginger and soy flavors, as well as being juicy and incredibly addictive. Enjoy them on their own, in soups, in raw or cooked noodle dishes, stir-fries, or as a garnish or side dish.

INGREDIENTS

2 cups (140 g) dried shiitake mushrooms

½–1 cup (200 g) sweetener of choice (you can use raw sugar, raw honey, or maple syrup)

1 cup (225 ml) light soy sauce or tamari

1 cup (225 ml) sherry vinegar

2 pieces ginger (about 2 inches/ 5 cm each), peeled and roughly sliced

1 Place the shiitake mushrooms in a large bowl and cover with hot water. Cover the bowl with a lid or flat plate and let mushrooms soak for about 15 minutes.

2 Drain the shiitakes, reserving the water, then trim and discard the stems. Thickly slice the caps.

3 Strain the water in which you soaked the shiitakes and reserve 1¾ cups (about 450 ml).

4 In a medium pot over medium heat, add the strained water, sweetener, soy sauce or tamari, sherry vinegar, ginger, and shiitakes. Bring to a boil, then lower heat. Simmer for approximately 30 minutes, stirring occasionally.

5 Remove from heat and allow to cool to room temperature. Discard the ginger (or save it to use in other dishes, like stir-fry). Remove the shiitakes, packing them in a quart (1 L) jar. Cover with the 1¾ cups (about 450 ml) reserved liquid.

6 Serve immediately or store in an airtight jar in the refrigerator for up to 1 month.

VEGGIE STOCK POWDER

Makes a 16-oz (1 pint) jar

This recipe is great for saving time when making a tasty soup (or stew or sauce), in the easiest way possible, without having to make broth and guard the stove for hours.

VEGETABLES

2 large carrots, thinly sliced

2 medium parsnips, thinly sliced

2 celery ribs, julienned

1 large potato, thinly sliced (I used a white sweet potato)

1 medium onion, thinly sliced

2 medium tomatoes, thinly sliced and pat dry (try to absorb as much moisture with a paper towel)

4 mushrooms, thinly sliced

2 red cabbage leaves, chopped into small pieces

1 large handful parsley (with stalks)

2 medium garlic cloves, thinly sliced

SEASONINGS

2 tsp sea salt flakes

2 tsp ground turmeric

1 tsp dried dill

½ tsp freshly cracked black pepper

½–1 tsp chili flakes (optional)

⅓ tsp ground nutmeg

1   Use a paper towel to absorb any extra moisture from the sliced vegetables.

2   Arrange all ingredients for vegetables on dehydrator sheets, in a single layer. You'll need about 6–7 sheets.

3   Dehydrate at 135°F (57°C) for 1 hour, then continue to dehydrate at 115°F (46°C) for up to 6 hours. Please note that vegetables such as potato, carrot, parsnip, and parsley, will be ready sooner than cabbage, tomato, celery, and onion. Check them after 2–3 hours and take out those that are done (moisture free).

4   Once all vegetables are done and completely moisture free, allow them to cool.

5   Add them to a blender or food processor and process until you get a fine, crumbled mix. You may need to do this in 2 batches.

6   In a large bowl, mix your ground veggies with all of the seasonings.

7   Store in an airtight jar in a cool, dry place in the pantry.

Tip: Slice all vegetables to about the same thickness, at or less than 2–3 millimeters. And to make slicing easier, use a mandolin.

NAPA CABBAGE KIMCHI

Makes 4–5 quarts (4–5 L)
Cooking time: 2 weeks (of waiting)

Although kimchi is readily available in stores, it is so much more rewarding to make yourself. It is easy to make, inexpensive, and all-natural. Plus, you can play with flavors to suit your taste. This is a basic recipe that you can build on as you start experimenting more. You can try it not only with napa cabbage, but also with daikon radish and cucumber. A grated beet will turn your kimchi pink, while red cabbage or a couple of purple carrots will add wonderful light purple hues. I also like this recipe because it uses no sugar, just a couple of sweet apples.

CABBAGE

1 medum head napa cabbage

2 tbsp coarse sea salt, divided

2 medium carrots, julienned

4 green (spring) onions, cut lengthwise in 1¼-inch (3 cm) pieces

PASTE

2 small sweet apples (or 1 medium), cored and finely grated (almost to a puréed consistency)

6 medium cloves garlic, finely grated

2¾-inch (8 cm) piece ginger, peeled and finely grated

5 tbsp Korean chili powder called kochukaru (if you can't find that, use 2 tbsp/7 g chili flakes, though final color and consistency of paste will be different)

¼ cup (60 ml) soy sauce or tamari

¼ cup (60 ml) water

1 Halve the cabbage lengthwise, then slice each half crossways in about 1-inch (2.5 cm) thick pieces.

2 Place the thicker cabbage pieces at the bottom of a large glass or plastic container and toss with 1 tablespoon sea salt. Massage for a few seconds. Add remaining cabbage slices and the remaining salt, and massage it all together for a few seconds.

3 Cover the container with a lid and place in the refrigerator overnight.

4 The following day, drain the cabbage, gently squeezing to remove excess water, and return it to the container. Add the carrots and green onions.

5 Place all paste ingredients in a large bowl and mix together until the consistency is paste-like. If the mixture is too thick, add a little water, 1 tablespoon at a time, until it becomes creamy like a salad dressing.

6   Add the paste to the cabbage mix and toss until thoroughly coated. You can massage it for a minute to make sure the flavors are evenly distributed and that the paste is absorbed in all the right places. (It's best to use food prep gloves to massage, as the garlic, ginger, and chilies can be harsh on your hands.)

7   Tightly pat the cabbage down and place a large plate on top to hold it firmly in place. Doing this will help it release more of its juices.

8   Tightly cover the top of the container with a layer of cling wrap, then seal it with a lid. The extra layer of cling wrap should ensure that your refrigerator will not smell. Place the container in the refrigerator.

9   Kimchi can be ready to eat in as little as 24 hours, but the flavor will be better after 1 week, and at its best after 2 weeks. The kimchi is best enjoyed within 4 weeks after making it. After that it will still be edible, though flavors will intensify and get stronger.

ZA'ATAR

Makes ²/₃ cup (66 g)

This traditional Middle Eastern spice blend is intensely aromatic and can be used to flavor everything from salad dressings, sauces, and salads to raw crackers, activated nuts and seeds, roasted vegetables, and baked bread.

INGREDIENTS

¼ cup (36 g) dried sumac

2 tbsp dried thyme

1 tbsp sesame seeds (raw or toasted),
    finely ground with a mortar and pestle

2 tbsp dried marjoram

2 tbsp dried oregano

1 tsp sea salt flakes

1　Place all ingredients into an airtight jar, secure with the lid, and shake well to combine.

2　Store the mix in the jar in the pantry for up to 3 months.

TWO-INGREDIENT NICE CREAM

Serves 2

During the summer, there's nothing better than cold, gooey, rich, creamy nice cream, topped with crunchy nuts and seeds, fresh fruit, cinnamon or nutmeg, and devoured within seconds. To make beautiful, sweet nice cream, it's best to use overripe bananas. Yes, the brown, spotty ones!

NICE CREAM

2 ripe bananas, peeled and cut into chunks

½ cup (120 ml) almond milk (or a nut or seed milk of your choice)

TOPPINGS (OPTIONAL)

Chopped nuts

Seeds

Cacao nibs

Chocolate drizzle

Ground cinnamon

Coconut sugar

1 Freeze the banana chunks in an airtight container for at least 2 hours or overnight for better results.

2 Add the frozen bananas to a blender or food processor with the almond milk and blend until creamy. Stop and scrape the sides down as necessary.

3 Serve immediately with your favorite toppings.

INDEX

ABOUT THE AUTHOR

CHRIS ANCA loves developing healthy and delicious recipes, and started keeping track of her culinary creations on *Tales of a Kitchen* (www.talesofakitchen.com), her popular blog that she started in 2011. Featuring loads of nourishing recipes, including a large selection of raw and vegan meals, she also owns Raw by Chris, a raw and organic catering business in Australia that specializes in delicious, guilt-free foods designed to nourish you from the inside out. Her most popular recipes are the "vegetable noodle" recipes she makes with her spiralizer, which inspired *Nourishing Noodles.*

Chris has appeared on national television, and she was the winner of the People's Choice Award for Voices in 2014. She has also been voted one of the Top 5 Food & Well-Being bloggers in Australia. Her recipes have been featured in many places, including *Fitness Magazine*, The Huffington Post, *Raw Food Magazine*, *Women's Health*, *Redbook Magazine*, The Kitchn, Relish, BuzzFeed, Greatist, *Chickpea Magazine*, and more.